The

TOMMY TYCHO

Story

Music, Maestro Please

BROLGA
PUBLISHING PTY LTD

Published by Brolga Publishing Pty Ltd
ACN 063 962 443
P.O. Box 959, Ringwood,
Victoria 3134, Australia.

National Library of Australia
Cataloguing-in-Publication entry

ISBN 0-909608-31-8

Printed by Griffin Paperbacks, Adelaide.
Design and Production by Pro Art Design, Adelaide.

ACKNOWLEDGEMENTS:

I would like to express my thanks to Mark Zocchi for finding my story interesting enough to be written and to Elizabeth Lohmeyer who patiently transcribed countless hours of tape despite my charming broken accent. Thanks also to Lolla Stewart and Julie Capaldo for their careful editing.

I would like to thank Florence Miles-Waldman and also Ken Laing for standing by me and guiding me through the occasional turbulence. Above all, I would like to thank Eve for putting up with a mad musician for 45 years.

Contents

Chapter 1
The Early Years

Since I was born, I have been surrounded by music. Not just any music, but the right kind of music.

It may seem odd to say that, but hearing good music played well by a big ensemble is something that a lot of people no longer experience or appreciate. Most people are musically illiterate simply because they have never been exposed to good music. Many people are unfamiliar with the sound of a symphony orchestra, which to me is the biggest instrument in the world. They hear orchestral music underscoring ads and films, they hear a trio and think of it as a band. To hear a full symphony orchestra on stage and to feel the power of the sound – it is like a tidal wave. It is an amazing experience and it is one that I was lucky enough to grow up with.

My mother was a celebrated soprano. Her name was Helen Tehel. She had been a member of the Vienna State Opera and the Budapest State Opera before her marriage and as a baby I was dragged along to concerts, the opera and to the operetta stages. I was spoiled rotten from the word go, surrounded not necessarily by classical music but good high quality music played well.

My mother was the sixteenth child in her family (I think that had something to do with the fact that in those days there was no television and no electricity so there was not much to do after dinner). She was the youngest and by the time she was born, her oldest sister also had a child with whom she shared a crib.

I do not recall more than a few of my mother's sisters. I know that my grandfather was a dairy farmer, he was not poor but not rich either. Most of his children remained in the country and continued as farmers with the exception of five of them who migrated to the USA. This branch of the family has since become a big group.

There is only one story that I can recall about my mother's mother and this would have been related to me by my older sister.

After my mother had been born, so the story goes, my grandmother walked out into the field one day and, overcome with the burden of so many children, she fell on her knees and prayed, 'Please God, no more!' Her eldest daughter who had followed her, tapped her on the shoulder and said, 'Mother, don't pray to God, pray to father!'

Whichever prayer it was – it worked. There were no more children after my mother.

My mother had an aunt, who was a celebrated operatic soprano in her day. I cannot recall her name, but I would assume this was around the turn of the century. As a child, mother must have shown some early desire and talent for singing because at the age of eight or so she accompanied this aunt on one of her tours of Europe. My mother, exposed to the world of touring and music, caught the bug. They returned to Hungary when she was about eighteen and she was enrolled into the Budapest School For Actors, which would have been the equivalent of the National Institute of Dramatic Arts in Australia. From there she went onto a singing career.

I presume that mother was the only one of the sixteen children with talent. It was certainly unusual for the times for her talent to be nurtured. Even when I was a child, the *pater familias* was still very much in existence in Europe.

It would have been even more so in her time. The father was the head of the household and the breadwinner. The mother stayed at home, cooking and washing and looking after the children. So it was really exceptional that mother sang, that her own family had nurtured her talent and allowed her to pursue a career on the stage.

Musicians and singers, people who performed on stage, were looked down on. I don't think this was an attitude unique to central Europe but it was particularly prevalent there. Entertainers were thought of as drunks, people of loose morals, the women little better than prostitutes. Unfortunately, most of the time it was true. But even when it wasn't and they were top class performers, there was still a stigma about being on the stage.

My father was not musical himself although he was a music lover. He was born in Vienna to a very wealthy and respected family. He was disowned by them when he married an entertainer and had to work for his living. He must have been good at his work because he became the General Manager of the Hungarian Electricity Commission which was privately owned at that time.

I loved my father but he died while still a young man in his forties. He had sustained an injury during World War 1 and later developed thrombosis which caused his death. I was very young at the time, about nine.

I remember I was never punished or hit by him. I think that was unusual, because as a rule, fathers in that time and culture were firm disciplinarians. I don't think he believed in corporal punishment. There is a story about him that was related to me by my mother and my sister; I do not recall this myself.

In Europe it is customary to have the main meal at midday. The whole family comes home and eats together.

As a child I was constantly daydreaming and, on this occasion they tell me, the spoon stopped midway to my mouth and I stared into space. I don't know what I was dreaming about – it was probably music. This in itself was not uncommon and usually father or whoever was talking to me would call, 'Tom' to bring me back. On this day when father called 'Tom' it didn't register. He said it again and it still didn't register, so then he thumped the table so hard I nearly shat myself. It was the only time I can remember hearing of him being aggressive.

Because I lost my father when I was so young, I do not remember very much about him. What I know is largely what I have been told by my mother. I resemble him in many ways. He was evidently a very serious man, bordering on melancholy. I don't know why but that was his nature, and I seem to have inherited something of that from him. Fortunately, I inherited far more of my mother's vitality and energy – a real show business personality.

I do remember my paternal grandmother. As far as I could ascertain, she was not a nice lady. I recall my father taking my sister and myself to visit her. My grandfather had died before I was born and she had, to some extent, mended the rift with my father. She was living in Budapest but, having come from Vienna, she spoke German. She refused to speak a word of Hungarian. As was common in middle-class families, my sister and I had learnt several languages including German which we were expected to speak to her. It was a very official kind of visit, we were all dolled up, presented and spoken to for about five minutes and then dismissed. She was an imperious old woman with a demanding and aggressive manner. She terrified my sister and myself but being well brought-up we, of course, behaved impeccably.

There was a lot of warmth in my family. The family unit

– my mother, father, sister – and myself, was very strong and I was close to them all.

I had an unusual childhood. I don't think I was ever a real child because I discovered music so young. That world was more real to me than the normal world of childhood. It is still what I love best about my early years – the culture, the music.

I grew up in Budapest which is really two cities joined by the Danube: Buda which is hilly and more well-to-do, and Pest which is flat . We lived in a beautiful house on the Pest side which had many rooms and even a swimming pool. We also had two cars which was an unheard of luxury in those days, and I was often driven to school.

When I think of my childhood, I think of music. Always, there was music. One of my earliest memories is of one of the first broadcasts on Hungarian radio. It was a special occasion and my mother was singing an aria which I later learned was Santuzza's Aria from 'Cavalleria Rusticana' (Rustic Chivalry). I was sitting on my father's knee listening to my mother's voice coming from a big old wireless and I could not comprehend it. I kept on asking my father where mother was, and was she really in that box?

My mother made a number of recordings early in her career. Following the custom, she did not sing much after she had children; caring for her family came first. There were occasional events that she did sing for however, and then she would disappear for a period of time to practise.

Because she had been a celebrated performer, she kept contact with a lot of artists and musicians and there was a constant stream of interesting visitors and dinner guests through our house. In those days, children were meant to be seen and not heard, and so we were usually sent to bed soon after dinner. But again, from what my mother and my sister tell me, I was a stroppy kid who objected to this and insisted on staying. My presence was tolerated, and so I was often allowed to sit under the piano and listen. The memories are hazy; all I remember is that those nights were magical – people were arguing animatedly, there were discussions about art and music and suddenly someone would jump up and race to the piano to demonstrate what they were talking about.

My sister, Marianne, remembers far more than I do, not just because she is older but because she has lived in Budapest all her life. With the distance in time and years, much of my childhood is forgotten. Marianne is twenty months older than I am and like all middle-class girls she started learning piano, as well as deportment and languages, from an early age. When she began piano lessons she was five and I was three and I threw a tantrum. 'How come she can learn?' I demanded. Mother said, 'But you can't even reach the pedals.' It didn't shut me up and eventually, just to humour me I suppose, she let me learn too. We were both taught by the same lady, a woman who lived around the corner, and within a couple of years I had outgrown what she could teach me. I guess it was about that point that mother and father recognised my talent. I was a child prodigy and that is an awful thing to be, I can tell you. I didn't want to do anything else; from the moment I discovered music I became consumed by it. I certainly wasn't "pushed" by my parents. If anything, it was quite the opposite.

Father used to be the president of a soccer team. At one point, when I was about seven, he decided that I was too involved in music and that it would be good for me to 'get out and do something'. So he decided I should play soccer. It wasn't a successful exercise. Not only did I hate it, but having been drenched while playing one day, I contracted pneumonia which was often fatal back then. I had a long illness and was taken to a private hospital in Austria for six months to recuperate. The only recollection I have of that time is of sitting in a deck chair rugged up in the crisp, clear mountain air.

I have always hated the cold. When I think of Budapest and my childhood, that is what I liked least. The slush, the snow and the cold. There is a cold smell that I can still recall. The four seasons are very clearly defined in that type of climate. I have always disliked autumn – dying leaves that ended in the bare branches of winter. Spring was always upbeat again and I was alive when it was warm, in the summer. There were trees and grass and bushes and flowers. That's a strong recollection I still have, that I was always waiting for the first days of spring when the snow disappeared and there was a particularly fresh and lovely new smell coming, and it was possible to look forward to summer.

In the years since I left, I have been back to Budapest a number of times, fortunately most visits were in the summer. This was very deliberate planning, I couldn't take the winters there anymore. However, there was one time when, because of work commitments, I did arrive there in the middle of winter. I was still Musical Director of Channel Seven and the only time I could take out was between Christmas and the beginning of the season at the end of February, so I took my daughter Vicky with me for a holiday. It was bitterly cold – well below zero. Vicky had never seen snow and when we got out of the aircraft there was snow everywhere. She was delighted and ran around to pick it up and then shrieked in terror because it burnt. She has also hated the cold ever since – I think she may have inherited it.

When my father died, my mother was devastated.

Obviously there had been great love between them. She went into a depression that lasted for about two years. We were taken care of by my father's sister while mother was in and out of hospital. Then eventually, because of her inner resilience, she snapped out of it one day and decided that enough was enough. She couldn't mourn any more – there were two children to look after. The first thing she did was hire a very large apartment in a less affluent area and she sold the house. I remember it was a problem to fit all the furniture from the huge house into the smaller apartment. I also recall that there was a large superannuation, which for the first two years after my father's death was the same amount that he had earned, and then it went down to 60 per cent and then to about 40 per cent. But even the 40 per cent was more than enough in those days, and so until the war reached us in Hungary in 1941 we were well off.

I was eleven when mother picked up the pieces of her life and we moved across town to the apartment. I had just started the first year of high school.

I did not particularly enjoy my schooling. When I was young, I was terrified of the teachers. Not that they were particularly bad but because of that terrible disciplinarian attitude which prevailed in those times. If you did something wrong you had to hold out your hand and down came the cane. I remember the threat more than the execution of it because my mother warned them that if they dared do that to me she would come to the school and do the same to them. I can't imagine her ever doing such a thing but she was protecting my pianist's hands rather than sparing me from discipline.

The school system required you to go to kindergarten when you were three or four years of age for two years, and then elementary school for four years. After four years, if you were good enough, you were allowed to attend what was called the high school. Otherwise you could choose to go to a school where they would teach you a trade for four years, which is a very clever idea actually. The ones who qualified to go into high school were obviously the ones who would eventually become doctors, lawyers, architects, artists, diplomats and so on. I was a good student, in spite of my almost total neglect of my studies, and I sailed through into high school.

By then, music was the consuming passion of my life. I spent most of my time playing the piano. During the last couple of years I was with my music teacher, I could virtually play as much as she could. I went for lessons – I think it was twice a week – and I was given instructions to further my knowledge of reading music. There was also the usual tedious practise of scales which is really the most important part but for a kid going up and down the scales – boring! In order to make it a little bit sweeter I was given pieces, nebulous things. Within half a year I said, 'I want some new things.' So it elevated itself alarmingly to the point where, when I was about eight years of age, I was playing rather difficult Scarlatti and Haydn sonatas which were way beyond my years.

My teacher held end-of-year exams in the form of a concert at her house, and all the parents were invited to hear their kids play. I was the star pupil and was always chosen to close the performance because I was playing things way beyond my years and beyond the other kids too, even though some of the pupils were sixteen, seventeen and eighteen years of age. My skill was pushed along by my passion without me even being aware of it. I was not competitive, I didn't compare myself to the other students and think, 'Aren't I great': I just wanted to know more. I was never satisfied, I kept gobbling up whatever I could.

Because my sister could also play, we used to play four hands on the one piano at home. There are hundreds and hundreds of arrangements for four hands, these were printed in the old days in Europe, symphonies by Beethoven, Mozart, Bach, Wagner. My sister wasn't so keen on it. I was. I kept on pulling her to the piano and saying, 'Let's play some more.' I must have driven her crazy. Sometimes mother actually had to stop us at 8 or 9 o'clock at night because, left to my own devices, I would have kept playing half the night and bullied my sister into it as well. I was possessed by it.

By this time I had to have a new teacher. My mother saw that I had outgrown my current teacher and she said, 'Okay, what we have to do is get you to a real teacher.' There was a world famous Hungarian violinist Joseph Szigety. He travelled the world with his accompanist Egon Petri who, as well as being a pianist, was also an accomplished teacher. Egon came back to Hungary because he had had enough of the travelling gypsy life. He became a teacher of piano at the Budapest Conservatorium.

There were two big music schools in Budapest at the time. The Franz Liszt Academy was of a higher standard and quality, and the Budapest Conservatorium was on a slightly lower level. Because Egon was Jewish he was not allowed to join the Franz Liszt Academy.

This was before the war came to Hungary but anti-Semitism was not uncommon. Hungary had always been anti-Semitic because it was predominantly a Roman Catholic country and the Jews had always been considered a problem throughout Europe – they still are regarded in this way. So there was already this alarming wind of discontent, and people who were of Jewish origin couldn't hold major positions in offices or government offices, and with schools such as the Franz Liszt Academy they were simply not allowed to join.

Because of Egon Petri's incredible talent mother took me to him and I started to learn from him privately. He came to our house about twice a week and all of a sudden I was rocketing to piano virtuosity. He introduced me to music like Gershwin's 'Rhapsody in Blue', which was exciting and different to me. In Europe, we would receive these kind of things twenty years later, not two or three years after they were introduced into America. I performed this piece at my first public concert which had been organised by Egon and one of the professors at the Franz Liszt Academy. It was a concert to show off the students. I do not recall how it all came about but obviously Egon had said, 'Here is this young prodigy of mine. He should play,' which I duly did. At that time, I was about ten years old.

As I remember these events now, I am aware of how extraordinary my experience was. But at the time, none of these things affected me because to me it was so damn natural to play what I was playing. It didn't occur to me that being taken on by such an eminent musician was something exceptional. To me it was a natural progression. Although I was virtually on a par with him at times, in my perception and understanding it was never in my mind to think, 'Oh my God, I am so clever.'

Egon had travelled the world and he was an open-thinking person. He obviously recognised the talent that I had and we became friends – not mates, but friends. I still gave him respect – that's the way I was brought up. That was the moral background. But occasionally, he would say, 'Bring out those four hand arrangements. Let's play them together.' And I just thought, 'Here, we are going to play something really great together.' It never occurred to me for a second to think this was a great honour that this man should lower himself to my level playing 'Beethoven Symphonies For Four Hands'. He stopped me a million times and he would say, 'No, that's the wrong phrasing. That line is played by the French horn, its got to sound like a French horn.' He showed me how to play it, and even sang it sounding like a French horn, and I would emulate it. From then on, when I played that phrase it sounded in my brain as a French horn, not as a piano, and Egon would say, 'Right, that's it.' This is still with me, because when I orchestrate things I don't need the piano to check it. If it's for a French horn, I hear it as a French horn. This came from those lessons.

Let me explain about pitch. There is what is called "perfect pitch" and there is also "relative pitch". It is possible to teach relative pitch, but not perfect pitch. Perfect pitch is rare. It is when you hear a note and you can say, 'That's a B,' without having any reference to a piano or any instrument. You can hear the note in your brain and you know what it is. I don't know why that happens, but that's what it is. It's like having a computer in your head. When someone who has perfect pitch hears something that is out of tune it is like Chinese torture.

Relative pitch is when somebody is taught that this note is a C and the fourth note above it is the F. So they'll play the C and F and then play another note and try to work out what that note is. There is an Italian term for it, "Solfeggio" which is the relativity of starting from one note to work out what the other is. This is what kids learn in music schools.

I've got perfect pitch. I didn't realise this until I was about twelve. When somebody played something I knew what key they were in because I heard it. When somebody played a piece I could go to the piano and play it in exactly the same key and everybody would ask, 'How did you know that? You weren't even looking.' But that's perfect pitch. It can be developed into inner hearing where you don't have to have an instrument to write music, hence Beethoven – when he was deaf he wrote just as well as when he heard what he was playing. Because it was all inside.

When I start to write an orchestration I don't need a piano to check what key I'm doing it in or what notes I'm running. I hear it in my head and I know what the notes are. Like someone who has learned how to write letters and words, you don't have to go to a machine to check if the letter you need is an L or an R or a D, you just start writing. This is virtually the same. Because I have learnt how to write, I know the capabilities and the range of the instruments. I know how one instrument sounds and I can hear it, even when there are ninety instruments in my head – it's no different.

After a year or two with Egon he suggested I start learning harmony and counterpoint, composing and conducting. I thought, 'Yes! That's what I want to do!' I still kept playing the piano, because it was a joy, but by introducing me to orchestral music and the works of modern composers such as Ravel and Debussy, this man opened up my brain to a huge world of music that I had not really been aware of. In those early years, the piano was my instrument and I was totally focused on it, and then suddenly I discovered that there was more to music than the piano. That was my downfall. I started to compose a concerto for piano and full orchestra. It was dreadful.

There was an old colleague and friend of my mother's whose name was Leo Weiner and he was one of the three biggest names in music in Hungary. There was Bartók, Kodaly and Weiner. The first two are world famous as composers, although Kodaly is perhaps remembered best today for the theme used by John Williams the American composer in the movie, 'Close Encounters of the Third Kind'. Leo Weiner was a great teacher, although he wasn't a great composer. Mother rang him up and said, 'I've got a boy here who is fourteen years old and he has written a piano concerto. I want you to have a look at him and if, in your opinion, he is talented, I want you to teach him.'

So duly we went along to Leo's apartment and I was filled with great confidence. I was quite sure that apart from Beethoven's this piano concerto was the best ever written. I was presented to him, and mother sat there with me while he studied the score for about half an hour in total silence. Then he turned back to me and said, 'This is awful,' and I just died. Mother said, 'Yes, I know it is dreadful but are you going to take him?' He said, 'Yes, I will.' Obviously, because she was also a musician, my mother could see the signs of my talent. At the time, I was not fully aware of how highly Leo thought of my talent, but it is still an honour to me that this great man, one of the greatest musicians in Hungary, took me on as his pupil.

Leo and I were to have a long association and he was one of the most important influences in my life. Soon after he began teaching me, the war broke out and because we were both Jewish, we ended up doing forced labour together.

Chapter 2
The War Years

Because I was so preoccupied with my music, I can't say that I was very aware of much else happening around me; much less was I aware of the political climate. I was also sheltered by wealth and acceptance so that I didn't realise things were about to change until they actually did. I recall the occasion, when I came home from school to find my mother was crying. She said, 'Sit down, I have bad news for you.' It was the day that Hitler came out with this edict that anyone who had one Jewish grandparent was to be declared Jewish. That was in Germany and it quickly reached all the other countries under German control. It was the first sign of alarm for the Jewish population.

I understood Jewishness as a religion. My paternal grandfather had been a Catholic who married a Jew. And so, my father was Jewish, as was my mother, but both of them converted to Lutheran faith, which was the other major religious persuasion in Hungary. I had been brought up as a Lutheran and this whole problem with the issue of Jewishness was unfamiliar to me.

When I asked mother what had happened, she explained about the edict and said, 'Well, you are Jewish,' and I said, 'So?' 'But don't you realise?' she said. 'Realise what?' I asked. She patiently explained that under this edict I was classed as Jewish, but I couldn't grasp the significance of it. 'So what?' I kept asking. She said, 'It means you are going to be persecuted.' Still I didn't understand. 'You could be killed,' she said. To which I asked, 'Okay, what can I do about it?' Mother looked at me and shook her head sadly. 'You are amazing. You don't seem to realise what goes on.' For the whole afternoon and evening we talked, and she told me about the political implications of these things.

I was about fourteen or fifteen years old. I should have known what was going on but I didn't because I was so locked into what I was doing, so focused on my music. I had not directly been discriminated against. At school, I was a good pupil and popular because of my music – at every function they dragged me out to play the piano. I was accepted and liked by all the other kids. It never occurred to me that because of a difference in religious beliefs people would allow such atrocities as were about to happen.

When Germany annexed Austria, Hungary also became part of the Axis powers by its association in the Austro-Hungarian alliance. So the Nazis had an enormous influence on Hungary through the Hungarian Government. However, the head of the Hungarian Government, Miklos Horthy, was anti-Nazi and he minimised the effect of their influence. Although the war in Europe began in 1939, until 1941 we were sheltered from it. From 1941-1944 things got worse. Hitler's edict regarding the identification and restriction of Jews, which had already been in existence, was now enforced.

The Jews were centralised in pockets and herded into apartment blocks in clumps of ten or so in various areas of Budapest. This made it easier to locate them and transfer them to the ghetto eventually. Jews had to wear a yellow star sewn onto everything they were wearing, whether they were male or female. There was a curfew in place. It started at five o'clock in the afternoon and went until ten o'clock the next morning. During this time you could not leave your abode if you were Jewish. We had to scamper and run like hell to get food, and conduct the usual daily business between ten o'clock in the morning and five o'clock in the afternoon.

One afternoon I was running late and it was already past five o'clock, but I was close to home and as I rounded the corner I ran smack straight into an SS soldier. I thought, 'That's it – I'm finished.' Being caught out after curfew meant you were likely be shot on the spot. He grabbed me and got my identity card from me and turned deathly pale because his name was also Tycho. He was an SS officer who was related to me.

It was an incredible coincidence. I am quite sure that I would not be here today without him. He was in shock. He spoke to me in German and said, 'You can't be...' and I said, 'Yes, I am.' I knew the family background and I told him about my paternal grandfather who was born in Czechoslovakia, the Roman Catholic who married a Jew.

This branch of the family was far reaching and extended into Germany, Munich and Stuttgart and places like that, and one of them happened to be this SS soldier. He was totally devastated. This guy then came with me to meet my mother and after that, when I was occasionally taken by other SS troupes on the street and, in fact, when I was taken into forced labour, he was the one who kept on pulling me out. Eventually, we were all herded into the ghetto and then there was nothing he could do. He might have even been taken to the Russian front or whatever; we never saw him again.

Within a short space of time, every male who was not already conscripted, irrespective of age, from nine to ninety, were taken to do forced labour. We were used to help the Hungarian and German Armies to dig trenches and to do menial labour. They very simply said, 'Every male must be in the square tomorrow morning at six o'clock,' and we were taken away. There was the expectation of never returning. Every day was lived in terror.

Leo Weiner and I worked together in the forced labour battalions. During that period of time when we had to do awful things, and awful things were done to us, we became close comrades. Even though he was then in his sixties and I was a boy of about fifteen. At night, when we had the meagre meal served out to us, our talk was constantly of music. It was like we wrapped ourselves in the music to protect us from the horrors that were happening around us. People looked at each other as if we were two cuckoos, who, in these awful tragic circumstances, were talking about music.

In the last year of the war, 1944 the Nazis removed Miklos Horthy from office and invaded Hungary. Despite having also declared war on the Soviet Union, the first thing they did was set about the systematic elimination of the Jews. They took everybody from their houses, which wasn't very difficult, because in Europe (even today) you had to have an identity card, like the one that was to be introduced, the Australia Card which everybody objected to. Even if you moved from one street to the next into a different apartment you had to go to the local authorities and show that you were leaving that address and have your identity card changed. Everything was in it – your religion, age, height, colour, it was virtually like a passport.

So they knew where the Jews were living; it was no secret. They collected all of us and built a ghetto in an area of about one hectare, and we were all forced into living in this area and sharing the apartments because they kept on bringing in more and more people.

We Jews in the ghetto in Budapest were probably the luckier ones. Certainly luckier than those in the rural areas. Because there were less of them it was quicker and easier to collect them and put them into wagons and trains and send them straight into the concentration camps in Germany. They were eliminated within a couple of days. But because there was in the vicinity of 150,000-160,000 Jews in Budapest, that was a much bigger task. During this period of time the Russians were advancing into Hungary so the two things sort of clashed and we survived.

These are not good memories, but because it has been so long it has faded. I have had such a magnificent life; my brain selects things not to remember and they fade. Life is good now.

We were in the ghetto until the Soviet army "liberated" us from the Germans, but it was from the fat into the frying pan. The Soviets circled the whole of Budapest so that there was no escape. There were many thousands of Germans trapped in the city but they wouldn't give up. The apartment buildings were all attached to one another and the Soviets broke down the walls between one house and the next – just enough for a man to crawl through – with the Germans firing at them from the other cellar. This is how it went on, from house to house, in every street and every avenue for about two weeks. The Soviets were virtually advancing house by house and in the process they just eliminated the Germans. It was frightening.

The Americans kept coming in droves, dropping the bombs – it seemed like a thousand bombers a day. You could set your clock by it. At ten o'clock in the morning and ten o'clock at night they would come for a couple of hours. Thousands of planes – not one, or ten, or fifteen, or a hundred – it was never-ending. They were bombing Budapest. There were no military targets as the Germans occupied everything. And it wasn't only Budapest: they were going towards the east to the front, helping the Russians combat the Germans from behind. The Soviets came from one end and the Americans came from the other side, flying in from Italy. Actually they came up from the south across Yugoslavia into Hungary, then veered to the right, to the front. The sirens went on at ten o'clock and if they weren't there we'd just look at the clock and say, 'They're late.' It was comical. People became so immune to these things that it became a joke. That is the human spirit: they could joke about it.

One time, one of my buddies – a school chum of mine – and I were roaming the streets to find anything, food, scraps of food, stale bread, whatever. We were out just as the bombers came and I said to Peter, 'Let's go under. Let's not walk on the street.' He said, 'Come on, don't be such a sissy,' and I said, 'Oh, alright.' It didn't matter: we saw death and destruction so often that it didn't bother us. We felt if it happened to us, it happens to us – what the hell! And so the first wave went by, and then there was always two or three minutes before the next one. We were walking down the street and we could hear the drone coming up and I said, 'Come on, we are only two houses away from home.' He said, 'No, no, no. I'll stay here in the doorway of this big apartment building.' I said, 'Come on, it's only two doors down,' 'No, you go.' he said. I went on, only to hear the sound of a bomb hitting the apartment building: he was dead. Right there, the entire apartment building demolished, with him under it. I was only about fifty metres away from it all. These were daily occurrences. Destruction was the order of the day.

The Soviet "liberation" took us away from the Nazis

only to be harassed by the Soviet soldiers. They had to show their bosses, the captains and generals, how many prisoners they had captured. They had eliminated so many Germans that there weren't enough prisoners and so they took Hungarians instead, thousands of Hungarian men, tearing stars off indiscriminately. It meant nothing that these people, the Jews, had suffered already; they were taken to Siberia. They were taken prisoner because the Soviets had to show victory. All this, after we had survived so much already.

In Budapest there was no electricity, no water, no gas, nothing: a huge city with no services, just snow up to your neck. There was virtually no food at that point, so the Soviet soldiers opened all these very heavy, corrugated iron shutters on stores and shops. These shops had stores of tin food, things like that. And, of course, everyone behaved like animals, attacking these places and robbing them in order to keep alive. My sister and I went out and we joined the struggle to get as much of these supplies as we could. Of course, the age-old bartering system started. Our neighbours had a huge case of flour and the other had a huge case of fat and another one had tins of vegetables. They would say, 'Okay, I'll give you one tin of this for that...' and that was how it went on for three months because there was just nothing to be had otherwise.

My sister and I had to walk for hours and hours sometimes until we saw a soldier with a big crowbar forcing open a shop. There were thousands of shops in Budapest. On this particular day we were the first ones there and this happened to be a shop of chocolates and sweets. Marianne and I took a big box and found some rope to tie around it and we pulled it behind us in the snow knowing that there was some great value in it. As we were going home – it took us an hour maybe two hours to drag this bloody thing – another soldier was opening up another shop. It turned out to be a music shop. I stopped. My sister said, 'Come on,' and I said, 'No, no, I've got to go in there.' Nobody went in there, as soon as they looked into it and saw it was instruments they just went off because food was their priority. I went in and saw this gorgeous, huge brass tuba and dragged it home. I had to have that tuba. When I got home my mother looked at me and said, 'What am I going to do with this, cook it?' I had it for a couple of years; it was my prized possession. I then sold it. But that was just typical of my attitude to things. I was totally impractical. In those days I was a daydreamer, and to me that was the greatest value. Chocolate – to hell with that!

One day we were back in our apartment building where we had lived before the war and we were the only ones in the building. It was a four storey building with two apartments on each floor and we were on the first floor. A truck stopped in front of the house and a Soviet General got out. He looked at the house and as there was no devastation or anything – it looked like a proper house, he came up and burst through our door and tried to explain that it would now be the Soviet Headquarters. Mother, having travelled Europe with her aunt, could speak a bit of Russian, so she made herself understood. The General started embracing her because at least somebody was speaking Russian, and so we were in favour. He kept on bringing truckloads of food, truckloads of clothes – everything you could imagine. We were really the lucky ones. He occupied the floor above us for about two weeks and what a life we had – food, clothes, everything you could imagine. Then he was moved off to Germany or Berlin and he took everything – all the clothes, and all the food. That was their mentality. Heart of gold but once they left, everything went with them!

The General was not an educated man and he was unfamiliar with the plumbing in our buildings. One day he went out fishing in the Danube which was only about a hundred metres away. He brought the fish home and, to keep it fresh, he put it into the toilet. Of course it disappeared and he came down a minute later knocking on our door asking, 'Where's my fish?' Mother could not understand what he was talking about. He took her up and showed her. 'I put it there in the water,' he said, and mother said, 'That's not for that!' Can you imagine a General who has never seen a toilet in his life?

Most of the Soviet troops came from the steppes of Russia, behind the Ural Mountains. They were lovely people but were as simple as anything. They were crazy for watches. To them it was a status symbol. They grabbed every watch they saw. Some of them had fifteen watches on one arm and fifteen on the other. They were taking them back to Russia somewhere. On one occasion I even saw a soldier with a grandfather clock! He found it somewhere in a shop that he'd opened up with a crowbar. He saw this huge big clock and it was on his back and he was carrying it, determined to carry it back with him to wherever he came from.

Among all the horrors of war, one of the saddest parts was what happened to the animals. The Germans had eventually run out of gasoline and tanks and cars and so on, so they had confiscated horses from the peasants, and the horses died with them. Because of the winter snow, they were frozen. Then spring came, February, March and when the snow started to melt it was open slather for anybody who wanted to carve up the horses to eat. I ate horse meat for two weeks like everybody else. But to see that as a young man – the people with their big knives hacking into it – it is an image that has stayed with me. It was a nightmare that actually was real.

One of the things that has happened in my life, as a result of all those times, is that I have become very sombre. People sometimes think I am a sourpuss but I am not. Obviously, for my brain to function, it helps by blocking it all out. When I went and saw 'Schindler's List' I looked at it as analytically as anybody else who had been through it. It was accurate, but it just touched the surface of what it was really like. People were crying all around me, including my wife, everybody. People said, 'Didn't you cry' and I said, 'No, I lost those fears when I was young. I never cried since.' But now I think it did affect me deeply: I just wasn't aware of it.

It is not as if I was protected from the horror by having been so absorbed in my own world of music. If anything, it was worse. It was so shocking. I believe the result of it is my being melancholy or sombre. My music stopped during the war. There was this period of a year or so when I was pushed down to the level of an animal. A daily existence of survival was the thing. Music didn't exist. It was virtually like a boxer training but not getting to throw a punch.

Chapter 3
Hungary After The War

By mid-1945 things started to get back to normal. There was a lot of energy put into reconstructing life in Budapest. The authorities, as soon as they had the opportunity, had running water, electricity and gas. Shops and businesses reopened. People started to get on with their lives as best they could. I was almost eighteen and the next few years were to decide the future of my music career for me.

I returned to my studies with Leo Weiner. Although he didn't have much time to spare, he took me on as a private pupil. There is another enduring friendship from those days, a buddy of mine who is still in Australia, in Adelaide. He is now retired, but he was the Dean of the wind and percussion section of the Sydney Conservatorium and one of the five or six best clarinet players in the world. His name is Gabor Reeves. He is also the reason I came to Australia but that is another story. Gabor and I went to Leo to learn. Eventually Gabor dropped out to pursue his clarinet but I kept going to Leo during 1946 and 1947. Those years are probably the most valuable two years of my life as a musician. I owe that man an enormous debt.

I was accepted into the Franz Liszt Academy. My days were busy, first with schooling, which went from eight o'clock to two o'clock and after that I went to the Academy. I was learning at an incredible rate. I was also broadening my interests both musically and in life. Like the whole country coming to life after the war, I wanted to experience it all and there was a pressing need to earn money so I joined a band, the Filu Orchestra.

Because the human spirit needs to have relaxation and enjoyment, by the summer of 1945 there was already a little open air restaurant in one of the areas in Budapest, where people sat at roughly made wooden tables and chairs. There was probably some awful coffee being served. There was still hardly any food, only what was brought in by the Americans on a regular basis by plane. But the people were there at night and we supplied the music for dancing. That was my first "gig" as a musician, my first professional engagement: Gabor Reeves, who was playing saxophone in those days, a drummer, a piano accordionist and me. June 1945, fifty years ago.

We were really dreadful but because it was the first sound of music after this awful holocaust, people shut their eyes, or rather their ears. We were young musicians and it was all really very bland and very poor.

By the autumn of 1945, the American military mission in Budapest had built, in the cellar of their headquarters, a beautiful nightclub called the Pengo Club (Pengo being Hungarian for a dollar). They had established this military mission for about 300-400 officers and they brought Coca Cola, Hershey Bar Chocolates, chewing gum and records. Americans, wherever they went, took along all the luxuries of home. So, they also brought with them their music. Benny Goodman, Glen Miller, Harry James, the big band sounds on these huge big disks, which were called V disks. V for Victory, and they were the first long playing records made. They also brought printed sheet music direct from America and they were called Hit Kits – all the greatest of the day were there. Because I spoke English, I made contact with them and got all these pieces and started playing them in Budapest, and so we were really the king pin because we were playing the latest music from America. We played dance music and tried to emulate the jazz idiom of the greats in America and the American style of playing. From then on I was hooked.

This is where my musical career really started, and looking back now, I can see it as a path which diverged. If I had pursued a strictly classical path, who knows what may have happened in my life.

Leo's greatest sorrow was that I kept playing dance music at night. He said, 'You are destined to be much better and bigger, why do you do this?' I said, 'Leo I've got to earn money.' It was a necessity, because my mother and sister could not earn a living. The only thing I could do was play the piano. But more than this, I had a great feeling for dance music and jazz and I loved it. I took to it like a duck to water.

When I joined this band, Filu Orchestra, I was the first to arrive at orchestrations and arrangements – dance arrangements for a band to play. When I got the American records they said, 'I would like to hear such and such' which was totally alien or unknown to me although they all were known pieces like 'In the Mood'. So I copied the music off these V disks, playing them over until the needle eventually wore out the tracks. The arrangement was exactly the same as the original. The Americans were totally amazed, they just couldn't believe it. 'Where did you get the music?' they asked. But because I've got inner hearing and the perfect pitch it was natural.

Looking back it is quite staggering that I was able to write orchestrations and arrangements in this unfamiliar style without being shown how. What gave me the edge to be able to do it was having the discipline of a classical grounding. Jazz just came to me because I had the feel, the instinct for it. But it was enhanced 100 per cent by the fact that I knew what I was doing with harmonies. It was as close to doing it as the original because there was no sheet music of it available at the time.

Now for a jazz musician who did not have any background in classical training it would have been an impossible task. I'm saying the instinct of jazz is one thing, but what I had learned before I started playing jazz is what helped me, in fact, get where I am today. I have got such a vast knowledge of music in general, not just classical, but jazz, theatrical music, film music — the lot. That's because of the discipline with which I have learned it.

There are not many musicians who cross over between classical and jazz, and even fewer who can do it well. Andre Previn is one, and there it just about stops. Many people would argue Leonard Bernstein did but I disagree. Bernstein was as close to jazz as anybody but he really didn't swing because he was still heavily steeped in classics as a classical conductor. All his light music things are still classically based. Even 'West Side Story' is not a swinging piece of music. It is just popular music; it really doesn't swing. He's brilliant, don't get me wrong, but it's not jazz. Andre Previn started out as a classical pianist then was transported by his father and his family, because of the Nazi terror in Germany, to Hollywood where he picked it up, like I did. He found the jazz in himself and went with it because he had the talent to do it. And now he has returned to the classics and is a celebrated conductor of all the symphony orchestras around the world.

Which brings me to the point that if musicians start in the classics then go to jazz they can do it easily, if they have the talent to make the transition. If a jazz musician wants to do classics – forget it, it'll never work, it never does. This is because they don't have the groundwork that a classical musician has. Classical musicians have more studies to complete to even get to the point of coming out on the stage. A jazz musician, if he is a saxophone player or guitar or pianist or trumpet player can learn his instrument and play it damn well but that's where it stops, because it is all from ear and an instinct rather than from discipline and learning.

Jazz is a feel, an instinct that cannot be learned. You can perfect the harmonic structure as a jazz musician for improvisation but you cannot learn jazz. It's either in you or it's not.

And so, throughout that summer I continued to play dance music at night, and we got more popular. And we got better. That's when I learnt to play jazz, how it worked, how to behave on a stage. When I fronted up for lessons in the daytime Leo said, 'So what did you play last night?' and I said, 'You don't want to know!'

I continued with my music studies for another year, but increasingly now it was the jazz, the dance music, that attracted me. It was the money, the energy of the music, it was my future, and by 1947 I gave up my studies to concentrate on it entirely.

When I think back on Leo's influence on my life, I can't value it highly enough. At the time, I didn't realise how big an influence he was. Because we were already adults and because of what we had been through together in the war, we were virtually on par. I did not call him Maestro anymore, it was Tom and Leo. I was a fool, not realising the promise, talent, man, teacher and genius that he was. He taught me a lot of incredible things.

Again, this ignorance, this stroppy arrogance of youth that I regret now looking back. I really should have called him Maestro and not Leo, to acknowledge that I respected the enormous knowledge he had. A long time later, and before my mother joined us in Sydney in 1961, she would write letters to me saying that Leo was always asking after me and that she kept telling him I was doing very well. 'Still doing the rubbish music but doing very well!' Eventually I got a book that he had written which was in Hungarian which is my bible virtually. It's called 'Harmony and Counterpoint' and he dedicated it to me. So he was obviously proud, or he must have realised that there was some extra spark or something.

The war destroyed a lot of the old values, which was not a bad thing in some cases. There was a formality that was very stale. But there were also some good things that were lost too. It was after the war that the old things started to break up. I'm sorry they did because one of them was respect. That has gone out of society in the world largely. Except, as I can see, the orient still keeps it. I've seen it in Hong Kong, travelling on buses. Somebody old will get onto the bus and a kid will jump up and give them their seat. I'm not talking about stupid things like machismo, that I hate. I am all for equality as far as human values are concerned but some respect should stay. You should respect your elders irrespective of whether they are senile or not.

By around Christmas time the first recording studios opened their gates, and we were the first ones to make records. They were still the breakable 78s. I don't know how many of them we recorded but they sold like hot cakes. It was the first influx of luxury in Budapest which had been ravaged for four years during the holocaust. People were trying to catch up with life and that was the first step – to have records at home to play on the wind-up gramophone.

In that period of time, the radio, which was government controlled, also began to broadcast entertainment programs. It was in that first year that the band was transmitting broadcasts every week and we were recognised in the street by people who had seen us. We were like rock stars now – we were it. I was earning a fortune. For a young man, it was an exciting life and it seemed as if things were back to normal, back to where it had stopped, all of a sudden, in 1940.

It was a great life but it was still not an entirely respectable way to earn a living. This is something that still strikes me as wrong. There used to be a custom back before World War II that musicians only got a skeleton fee. The rest of it came from the "Baksheesh" that people threw on the plate next to the band as they left. That was a lot more money than what we were earning. I'm afraid it was the most degrading thing – like giving money to a beggar. That was the way it was but I could never abide that concept. It was something that carried over from before my mother's time, and still was evident in a subtle way. We were still "the musos" as I hate to call musicians. But we were virtually on a par with prostitutes and street cleaners and gangsters – musicians were never respected. People came and listened and they enjoyed themselves and said, 'That was lovely. Here, have ten dollars,' which I find awful. It's degrading. I don't know, maybe I'm wrong but I don't think I am.

After this second summer we went into the nightclub in Budapest called 'The Arizona'. There was a floor show with all the chorus girls and the full bit. In those days, aping and emulating the French was the "in thing" in Europe. These nightclubs opened up about ten o'clock at night until five in the morning, every night including Saturday and Sunday. We played dance music from ten p.m. until twelve midnight then there was a floor show which went an hour and a half to two hours: no stopping, no five minute tea break, nothing – you just went on. We grabbed food, and drank while we were playing. At two o'clock the dance music started. Then at about 3.00a.m. or 3.30a.m. everything quietened down and there were these little cubicles which had curtains and the chorus girls went in there to earn extra money entertaining gentlemen in private. All the major clubs in Europe were the same. The chorus girls used to be sitting by themselves or in pairs at tables, then they did the floor show, then they got changed and went back to sitting at the tables for display. A gentleman would ask for a particular girl to come and have a glass of champagne with him. Later they would disappear into a very elaborately designed and furbished cubicle which had all the amenities in the world. Very high class... the girls were providing "horizontal refreshment".

To soften up the lady, by the time the dance music finished about 2.30am, a few of musicians would be asked to come and play at the table and entertain the couple. This was also private entertainment, so you usually had extra money given to you. This degrading awful damn thing again! I do not think of this as being the most tasteful thing I have ever done but I had to do it, it was part of the job.

The contrast was not lost on me however, having come from appearing on a platform with the Hungarian Symphony Orchestra doing 'Rhapsody in Blue' at the age of about twelve to, at the age of eighteen, kowtowing to some absolute lowlifes and given money with a disdainful, 'Here you are. This is for your services.' I can remember wondering at times about the choice I had made. At that point I still had this grand idea of the future, that when I had amassed enough money I would go back to the Academy again and get my diploma – which I never did.

To be honest, the nightclub was an exotic environment

for a young man to be in. It was certainly an education in more than one sense. I learnt a lot about music there, I also learnt a lot about people and about life.

Initially, while I was working at the nightclubs, I was still going to high school. The late hours took their toll and of course my scholastic level was close to zilch but I still went on because I had to do it to get a final certificate. Until one day the headmaster happened to be at the nightclub. He saw me and I saw him, and he paled and I laughed because I thought it was not going to be a problem. In fact, when I had to go and play at a table, he was still there with a lady. When the lady excused herself he said, 'We are not going to talk about this are we?' I said, 'No.' It was a mutual agreement and I passed. Not because I was good – I just passed.

But best of all, I was learning to play music that I had never played before: learning the intricacies and complexities of accompanying a floor show, which is not easy, and learning to overcome the difficulties of choreography. It was still a matter of a band with me playing the piano, backing them and doing the right thing by them. There were singers who sang songs in different keys to the sheet copy, and in styles that they had acquired and so on – that was my apprenticeship. Although I wasn't the leader as far as the audience was concerned, I was virtually the leader within the band because I wrote the arrangements. I did the background, I did everything except be the frontman. By that time I knew how to orchestrate, I knew how to write music, and because of this meteoric speed at which I had acquired everything up to that point, I was ready – I was better than ready – at eighteen, to take on the world.

Chapter 4
The Middle East Adventure

In 1948, a Hungarian musician called Jules Szepesi who had been stranded in Teheran during the war years, returned from Iran. He thought he could live like a king because he had amassed a fortune during those four years in Teheran. He came home with two dozen suitcases filled with silver and carpets and goodies, only to find when he arrived back that, as he travelled from Teheran to the Soviet Union and then down to Budapest, all his goodies had been stolen and replaced with bricks. He opened up the suitcases finding nothing. No clothes, no nothing. Disenchanted, he made plans to return to Teheran.

He got in contact with the owner of the very rich and famous Park Hotel in Teheran and said, 'I've got this magnificent Hungarian show band on contract.' He didn't have anything, but he knew he could put a good band together like that. He got a contract and began to put together the band. Being a bit smart in this area, he only wanted to take unattached young males, and so I was asked 'How would you like to go to Teheran?' My mother looked at him and said, 'He is not going.' I looked at mother and said, 'Yes, Mother, I am'. She simply said, 'I'll talk to you after.' When he was gone I walked into the room and the first thing that I got was a sharp slap on my face. 'I tell you, you are not going.' I said, 'Mother, I am a grown person; I am going.' She said 'Well, okay, we will discuss it.' I replied, 'No, we won't! I'm going.' 'Why the hell do you want to go to Teheran and play in a band?' she asked. 'You are destined to do bigger, better things.' She wasn't thinking of the financial restraint it was simply that she was thinking of my future. 'You have done all this work and are you going to throw it away?' I said, 'No Mother, I want to see the world.' And that was the one thing she finally understood.

In furious tempo, I wrote orchestration after orchestration to build up a repertoire, and we rehearsed at our place. I remember the sense of anticipation. It was spring time and with the windows open there was a crowd of people down in the street listening to us rehearse upstairs. The contract didn't arrive and we kept asking 'When?' and kept on rehearsing. There were problems with passports and travelling arrangements. We had to travel through Yugoslavia, Greece, Turkey to get to Iran. There was no transport, there were no aeroplanes. So we had to go by train, by boat, by bus. It was a nightmare. It kept on being postponed until suddenly Jules triumphantly came one day with the telegram saying we were on our way. This was it.

My decision to leave Hungary had more to do with a young man's sense of adventure than with anything else, but in fact, in 1947, the political situation was looking ominous again. The Communists looked very much like the Nazis in different coloured shirts and I had no desire to become involved with them. In the months we were waiting to get our travel arrangements in order, I did a number of orchestrating jobs for the income more than anything and one of these led to an amazing offer. I was still only nineteen at this stage but it was suggested to me that if I became a member of the Communist Party, I would be offered the job of Musical Director for the National Hungarian Broadcasting Service. Although I was flattered, I had no real desire to commit myself to such a task; in hindsight, I believe my intuition was fortunate.

We all boarded the train to Belgrade, Yugoslavia, well rehearsed and with a couple of suitcases each. We arrived in Belgrade at nine o'clock the following morning. During the night Tito who was the leader of the Yugoslavian Republic, had declared war on Hungary. So as soon as we arrived in Belgrade we were arrested. We were kept in the wagon shunters beside the rail somewhere for one week. The Red Cross supplied us food daily. We were infested with lice because there were no washing facilities, there was nothing. Then finally, the hostilities ceased. The Hungarians patched up their troubles with Tito and we were on our way.

We got to Sofia in Bulgaria only to be taken off again. But this time it was because news had reached there that Tito and Hungary had conquered their differences and so we were wined and dined, and for the first time in fourteen days I had a shower. Then we were put on a train to go to Istanbul. That was the famous Orient Express which had the same line going from Paris to Istanbul and back. When we got to the little section which goes through Greece, which is about a half-hour trip, we were taken off the train again because the Greek Communists had blown up a bridge. There was no way for the train to cross and we walked from there to the next bus stop which was two kilometres, with all the suitcases. We boarded the bus and went past Greek territory into Turkey and we got onto another bus. Eventually, we reached a place called Erzerum in Turkey. What should have taken about forty hours took us two weeks.

As soon as we got to Istanbul, Jules cabled the Park Hotel. The Hotel answered saying they had arranged another band in the meantime – where had we been? We finally squared it by saying we had all these troubles, and they said, 'Well look, you stay in Istanbul for two weeks while this band plays out its contract and then we will get some transport to get you across to Teheran.' So we lived the life of Riley in Istanbul at the Park Hotel's expense. Finally, aeroplane tickets arrived for all of us; we could barely believe it. The first flight by KLM from Amsterdam to Teheran, put down in Istanbul. We were the only passengers on the flight to Iran. We got to Teheran, the door opened and the forty-four degrees Celsius hit us. I will never forget it as long as I live. I walked down onto the tarmac and the tarmac was soft. The asphalt was burning. I thought to myself, 'What on earth am I doing here?' but I must admit that I got used to the heat very quickly.

In those days, planes were not the long-range jets of today, and a plane trip from Europe to virtually anywhere meant a series of hops from Istanbul to Teheran, from Teheran to Karachi, Karachi to Calcutta, Calcutta to Hong Kong and then Tokyo. It was a long trip and it was all stops. Teheran was a key refuelling stop. Everybody you can imagine who travelled to the Orient – businessmen, artists, all travelled through there.

The Park Hotel was a brilliantly furbished, lovely five star hotel in Teheran. This is where we were contracted to play and, of course, being European, we were something of a novelty. The opening night was like a royal command performance and we were treated like stars. The Park Hotel was chic and definitely the "in" place to be.

I loved the attention we were getting playing at the Park Hotel. It was the first time that I started to feel this theatrical adoration and I loved it. And I haven't stopped loving it since. It spurs you on to do whatever you do and do it better than before. I think that's what motivates a lot of performers – the true performers. They've got to get out there and show their wares and do it as well as they can. The attention we were getting everywhere was lovely.

Our normal routine was to start about 8.00p.m. and we finished up invariably after 2.00a.m. We started to play what was called "Palm Court" music. This was gentle background music originally played by a small ensemble while the people had afternoon tea and chatted. We played while the people were eating. It was a beautiful restaurant with a parquet dance floor. Then around 10.00p.m. we started to play dance music for an hour. Then the band did a floor show for about forty-five minutes featuring each musician in a different way. I played piano solo and the dance music went on until the last guest left, which could have been one, two or even three in the morning. In itself it was nothing new, except we were a little more experienced.

For a musician, the hours were lousy. Mostly, I adapted to them but there was one time when it got the better of me. We were playing on New Year's Eve and this was a first in Iran and so, of course, it was a big event and sold out weeks and weeks beforehand. The elite were there. We followed the same format and started to play music for them while they ate, and then the dance music started, and continued through midnight. Then we did a bit of a floor show and kept on playing dance music. We played until nine o'clock the next morning. I was so tired, all of us were absolutely buggered, so we staggered back home and slept. I woke up at six o'clock and I staggered out of bed into the shower and knocked on the door of the my colleagues. They looked at me and they said, 'You bastard.' 'What did I do?' I asked. 'You don't know?' they said. 'No.' I answered. They looked at each other – the same thing. I was public enemy Number One and I didn't know why. We got into the taxi, arrived at the hotel and I was still wondering what I had done. Then the band leader arrived and he sarcastically said, 'Thanks!' I was thinking this was either a gag or I'd done something really dreadful. And so we started playing but they were all very angry with me, and in the first break I went to the band leader and I said, 'Jules, what did I do?' He said, 'Oh come on!' I said, 'Come on, tell me. I don't know! I honestly don't know. Did I do something terrible?' He said, 'Yes you did.' I asked him what I had done. 'You weren't here yesterday,' he replied. I said, 'What do you mean, yesterday?' I had slept for thirty-two hours straight – I didn't even go to the toilet! I was dead to the world. They tried to wake me and nothing: they went and played without me then. I said, 'You're pulling my leg.' But he replied, 'Go on and look at the calendar.'

Iran was a curious place. Such a contrast between the rich and the poor. Because I was a European piano player, the rich people wanted to have their offspring taught by me. They were totally untalented musically but they paid me such huge fees that it didn't matter. I was picked up by various Rolls Royces, Jaguars, Bentleys or Cadillacs every afternoon after school finished and I kept on giving lessons to these totally untalented kids, and was wined and dined. I was earning unbelievable amounts of pay, apart from what I was doing at the Park Hotel.

There were these elite who were beyond opulence and then there was the complete opposite – poverty-stricken peasants and beggars. It was just incredible. You could not walk down the street without being accosted by hundreds on every corner. At first, my heart bled – I couldn't believe it; I kept giving money until somebody wised me up and said, 'Look, you keep giving money and they will follow you forever – so don't.' I objected. 'But look...' 'No, just don't.' I was told. Eventually, you steel yourself to it, ignore it and just keep walking. Then they leave you alone. But I never got over this vast discrepancy living side by side – this incredible wealth and unbelievable poverty .

The elite were educated in Europe because they had the money and because there were not enough educational facilities in Iran to broaden their spectrum and make a person of cosmopolitan approach. So all these moneyed people sent their kids to Switzerland, Paris, and London to study. When they came back they had that extra spark. First of all, they could speak three or four languages, and they had been to New York and they had seen this and that. It was a broadened outlook for these people but they were not interesting. They were just emulating, aping or copying all their peers of a similar stratum in the various other countries. They were not unique in any way.

The fact that the Ayatollah gained so much support does not seem so surprising when you consider that the people were basically very strong Muslims and actually hated the artificial sophisticated veneer. They hated the Westernised kind of outfit on women, and the lipstick – most of them liked to have the women's hair covered and nothing except the eyes showing. Deep down they were still Muslims and hated all the modern cosmopolitan behaviour. So when the Ayatollah came in, they reverted very quickly to what they believed deep down and wanted to happen. I was totally deluded by that because I thought they were Westernised people but they were not.

One night, as I was getting ready for a performance, the manager of the hotel and Jules came looking for me. Jules looked very serious and said I must go with him and the manager. I was hurriedly ushered out into a limousine that was waiting nearby. I didn't know what was going on and before I knew it I was being driven to the Shah's summer palace, where I was taken into one of the most amazingly lavish rooms I have ever seen. It was an enormous ballroom covered by a single gigantic Persian carpet. It would have been absolutely priceless. The Shah's Protocol Master informed me that I would be playing for the Shah and his guests, and gestured to my instrument – a piano accordion. 'But this is not my instrument,' I said, 'I play the piano, not the piano accordion.' He looked at me and said, 'Then you have one hour to practice'.

And so I played the piano accordion for the Shah and his guests. It was a long night. I played and I played and my arms were aching and they kept on dancing and I kept playing. Finally, the Shah himself danced past me. He must have seen my distress and he stopped and asked me what was the matter. I told him that I was a pianist and that this instrument was not my usual instrument. At the time he made some courteous response. The night finally ended and it took literally days for my poor arms to recover. Before long, I was again summoned to the palace, and I groaned and thought, 'Oh, no, not again.' But, do you know, when I walked into the ballroom there was a magnificent Steinway. And not just there. The Protocol Master showed me through all the public rooms and each room had a Steinway, each matched to the decor of the room.

Such opulence was just beyond belief. Much later, I was shown some other rooms in the palace. One of them was a type of state room where gifts for visiting dignitaries were housed. When I walked into that room I can only describe it as looking like a Hollywood prop room. It contained huge samovars and silver trays. One thing that I noticed was a cigar box, made from gold and weighing about five kilos. On it was carved a map of Iran and the cities were in diamonds. That was just one thing there amongst thousands of articles. It looked unreal to me.

I was also fortunate to actually meet the Shah. He was the most noble, regal looking person. The confidence that a person like that has – and I have seen this in other people, political leaders and great stars – they have an aura of confidence that just radiates from them. It's incredible, I can't describe it. I could call it charisma, it's something that is separating them from everybody else. The Shah had that. When I walked in he sat behind this enormous desk and I had to bow my head, because without saying a word he commanded that. Not only because he was the Emperor – I was told I had to bow when I walked in and I had to walk backwards when I walked out – he just radiated this enormous Something and he simply said, 'Please sit down.' It wasn't theatrical – when you see this acted by a person you say, 'Oh what a ham.' But it was natural: he was the head of a nation of fifty million people with a tradition of 2000 or however many years. The same thing happened in a much more subtle and quiet way when, many years later, I met the Queen and Prince Charles. It is inbuilt. Probably the tradition that they know, where they come from, just gives them this extra Something. I didn't see that with the young Prince Andrew, and I certainly didn't see it with Diana. But the Queen has this quiet, regal Something which radiates, and you are virtually compelled to bow down. The same thing happened to me when I met some of the big stars, like Frank Sinatra. He didn't have to say a damn thing. But I could sense it a mile away and everybody else can as well.

The contract with the Park Hotel was initially for a year but it turned into three years. They were interesting years for me and it payed well. Since the war my mother no longer received any of father's pension, as all of the previous agreements were wiped under the new government. So it was my job to support them. Before I left I took a huge advance which was a year and a half of my salary, from my band leader who had to get it from the management of the hotel from Teheran. I left it there in Hungary for them and I also discovered how to smuggle goods to them. I was warned that if I wanted to send anything it would be taxed in Iran and the Hungarian authorities would also put some extra excise duty on it. And so the best way to do it was to hide it. I would hide things in the lining of a suit. I kept sending all kinds of things, from watches to valuable rings and things like that.

I also learnt much musically in Iran, because my mind was fertile and open, and I heard this incredibly exotic music which is based on a different scale system to the western scale system. In the western scale, an octave is seven notes or twelve semitones. In contrast, the middle eastern scale has twenty-four quarter tones. I was fascinated by it. I even composed a violin concerto about six or seven years ago here in Australia based on those themes. It has never yet been played but there will be time.

The use of the quarter tones is very skilful. It is pitched properly but to us it sometimes sounds like it's out of tune. To them it's not. It sounds like that to us because our ears, since birth, have been regulated to the western scale and anything alien to that we just go 'Aaahh! It sounds wrong.' It is the same with Chinese music. The fact that it sounds repetitious is because it is very simple music. I can't describe it any better – it hasn't got the sophistication of development of European music. Compare the development of European music, starting with Palestrina back in the fourteenth and fifteenth century, and then go to people like Vivaldi and Scarlatti and then Bach and so on – it just grew and became very sophisticated. In contrast, middle eastern music stayed on the same ethnic level – nothing changed.

I met a lot of Persian musicians and that's how I learned how they do these things. I can't do it because I'm not trained to and I didn't even bother to put energy into trying to emulate it. But I could see what happened there and it was fascinating, musically speaking.

We could have stayed with that contract at the Park Hotel forever, but eventually, Jules accepted a better contract to go to Baghdad to another nightclub, and I thought, 'Here we go again.' I had just about had enough of the nightclub scene although the money was good. More importantly though, by this time I was already courting Eve and we were planning to marry.

Eve's family was Hungarian but we met in Teheran. Her father was an engineer who was working for the Shah, the father of the last one who was overthrown. Until 1935 the country was called Persia, and this Shah was trying to establish a new order to bring it out of the middle ages into the modern era of Iran. And so he encouraged a lot of European doctors and teachers and engineers and such people to go there. Eve's father was one of these and so the family moved there in about 1937 and so, fortunately, missed the horrors of the war in Europe.

Eve learnt Persian. She went to a French convent school and so she also learnt French In fact, she is something of a linguist. She speaks, in total, half a dozen languages. Her mother was musical and from her Eve inherited a fine singing voice. The two of them performed in concert together occasionally. Her family came to the Park Hotel regularly. I may have seen her there before but

I can recall when I first noticed her: she was dancing with her uncle. I was watching from the piano and they danced past me. I did not know who she was then, but it was love at first sight. I did not speak to her then, and I had no idea what nationality she was. Imagine how thrilled I was when, soon after that, I walked past their table and heard them speaking Hungarian.

Some time later, she was approached by His Masters Voice to make a recording and her family asked me if I would accompany her. And so that is how we got to know each other. I was invited to her parents' place for Christmas, and that's when I told her how my eyes had sparkled when I saw her dance past me and that I was in love with her. This was the time when the band was taking up a new contract in Baghdad. I asked Eve to marry me and she accepted. A few weeks after I arrived, she joined me there and we were married. I realised then that I had had enough of the gypsy life and I decided it was time to settle down. That seemed like an easy decision but it was not without complications.

Eve had been married before and she had a young daughter, who was then about four years old, called Dory. When Eve was aged sixteen or seventeen she had fallen in love with this hugely handsome Iranian who was also a multimillionaire. She married him and only afterwards realised her mistake. By then she was pregnant with Dory but luckily she had, for no real reason, kept her Hungarian citizenship and passport. Without it, she would have been bound to him by Muslim law, but because of it she was able to divorce him, which she did, to his great anger. It was not so much that there was animosity between them but more that he was handsome and wealthy and he was a playboy. Eve was a young woman and her illusions were shattered when she discovered he did not share her ideal of a monogamous marriage and so she chose to end it.

We had, by this time, worked for about ten months in Baghdad. I was playing every night and I felt like I had no future. Our contract was due to finish and I knew it was time to move on. Jules came in one day and announced that he was teeing up a magnificent contract for the band in Bombay at one of the best hotels there, the Taj Mahal. At the same time I had just received a letter from my old friend Gabor Reeves who was already in Sydney. He had written to me saying how great the place was and he urged me to come to Australia. It all just came together for me at that moment and I said to Jules, 'I'm sorry but I'm not coming with you.'

He begged, cajoled, intimidated, threatened me – you name it. And once he realised that I obviously had made up my mind, that I was not going, he then wanted to kill me – he really did. I guess that finding a replacement pianist in the middle of nowhere who also had my arranging and composing skills was difficult. But he was a vindictive man and he got his revenge on me.

We cannot prove it but we still believe it was the malice of this guy, Jules, which was behind what subsequently happened. Whoever it was, someone wrote to the man who was Eve's first husband telling him that we were living in Baghdad with Dory and we were about to go to Australia. Until then he hadn't bothered with us. He was a gay blade, living it up, dancing around with more girl friends than he had hairs on his head. But being a typical macho man and Muslim to boot, it irked him. Two days before we were due to leave for Sydney he came and took Dory away. We were both desolate but there was nothing Eve or I could do about it.

Being in a Muslim country meant we had not a leg to stand on. Added to this was the fact that he and his family were one of the wealthiest and most elite in Iran. But even if he was an ordinary Iranian I wouldn't have had a chance with him. So we left, even though it broke Eve's heart. Dory was brought up mostly by her grandmother, and she and Eve stayed in constant contact by letter. But it was nearly eleven years later when Dory, then a teenager, was sent to London for schooling, that they saw each other again.

I regard her as my own daughter and she regards me as her father. She since has married an Iranian and has two daughters and a grandson, and so we are great grandparents as well. She visits us regularly, and spends a fair amount of time here in Australia. Our oldest granddaughter, Bita and her little boy are out here at the moment. Over the years, we have spent a lot of time together; from a distance of many miles, it has worked out and in my mind, clearly there is no difference between Dory and Vicky, my younger daughter. I love them all dearly, and the granddaughters and the little great grandson are as my own – to me there is no difference. That is the family heritage that I brought with me from central Europe – the family is virtually sacred.

At the time though, it was devastating. The trip from Baghdad was like a nightmare. We went by train through the desert to Basra, the northernmost point of the Persian Gulf, where the oil is in Iraq. We stagnated there for about two weeks because, right at that point, the first oil trouble started and all the foreign staff of the oil companies – English, French, Americans, and Germans – were evacuated instantly. Every available ship, train, car, plane was occupied. Eventually we heard that there was a chance of a plane going from Baghdad to Karachi. We went into the Thomas Cook office and bought tickets. They cost £500 each, this is back in 1951 and this was about all the money I had. We had intended to use it to set us up in Australia. We went back to Baghdad, got on the plane, and came to Karachi. Then from there we flew to Calcutta, stayed overnight, then flew from Calcutta to Singapore. In Singapore we stayed overnight at the Raffles Hotel which was an absolute dream, like being in a movie set, and then we flew on to Jakarta, Darwin and finally Sydney. It took us five days and five nights.

Chapter 5
Australia

We put in an application to emigrate to South Africa, America and Australia, and Australia responded first. I've not regretted it for a second. Well, that's not entirely true. When we landed in Darwin, for a moment there, I did wonder what Gabor had been on about. But it was momentary, and once we landed in Sydney, I knew this was my home.

I sometimes wonder what would have happened in my life if I had gone to America. I daresay I would have been able to pursue a fairly high profile career. Maybe there it would have been even quicker than here in Australia – I don't know. But, no doubt, I would be six feet under now because of the pressure. The pressure in the American music business is unbelievable. I love Americans, don't get me wrong but the Americans have got one God and it is the almighty dollar. I'm not talking about rock singers or rock stars. I'm just talking about people like me – conductors, arrangers, Hollywood film writers and so on. They live like dogs.

On one particular occasion I went to Las Vegas to visit a friend there, Bob Crosby, Bing's brother, who had a famous Dixieland band 'Bob Crosby and the Bobcats'. Bob came out here and did a television series with me and we became firm friends. While I was there one day the owner of the hotel came and sat down with us to have a drink. Bob introduced me as the Maestro from Down Under. The guy asked, 'Would you like to work here?' I thought, Well, why not? This was 1962 and he offered me a starting salary of $10,000 a week. Unbelievable money! But he also said, 'We've got three shows a night, seven nights a week and after one year you can have a three week holiday.' I said I would think it over. I talked to Eve about it and ended up saying, 'No thanks.' That was just as a conductor of an orchestra. In Vegas these were the figures; big performers would earn $1,000,000 a week. These were telephone numbers, so what was ten thousand bucks? But I just thought, No, I couldn't. As for the American scene, I'm glad I have lived here and not there.

When I first got to Australia, like any young man with lots of cocky confidence and talent, I thought it would be a piece of cake. However, I found it was not going to be so easy.

My friend Gabor and his wife waited for us at Mascot Airport and, thinking that I would be coming from the Orient with loads of money, they had booked us into the Carlton Hotel in Castlereagh Street in Sydney. In actual fact, Eve and I had about £45 to our name. We had very little luggage, and all of our possessions fitted into six suitcases which would arrive on a ship some ten months later. The Carlton cost about twenty-five guineas a night but we stayed that first night because it was already booked. We moved out the next morning and into a little guesthouse in Bondi and stayed there. We arrived there on Saturday morning and on Sunday Gabor and his wife left for Brisbane to work for the Queensland Symphony Orchestra. And so the two of us were on our own.

When we first arrived and we saw Sydney we were like the little country bumpkins who came up into the big smoke. Coming from the Orient, this was heaven – this was paradise. Being able to speak English, although not as well as I do now, we had no trouble communicating. Gabor said to us, 'Now on Monday morning you get onto this tram and go into the city and you go and apply for a job at David Jones.' I said, 'What is a David Jones?' He said 'It's a store and they are always looking for people to work. Just to tide you over until you get onto your feet, go there.'

On Monday morning we got onto the tram, went into the city, and into the David Jones store. We went up to the fifth floor, to the staff manager's office. We were told that they were looking for sales people, so Eve decided to give it a try. She had to fill out an application form and eventually she was called into the office. When she came out she said, 'I got the job, I'll see you at six o'clock at the staff door entrance down here.' I was about to leave when a girl at the counter asked, 'Excuse me, are you also looking for work?' I said 'Yes, I guess I am.' Until then, I really had no concept of working outside of music. I filled out the form she offered me and I went in to see the staff manager, a very courteous man who asked me what work I had done. I said, 'I am a musician.' He looked at me and said, 'I'm sorry but we don't have positions for musicians. There's a vacancy at the moment at the Elizabeth Street receiving dock as a labourer.' 'What do I do?' I asked. He explained. 'Well, it is very simple. These big trucks come in and deliver goods which you put into big baskets on wheels and you have to take them to the various departments and empty the contents and put them onto the shelf.' 'What am I called?' I asked. He replied, 'You're a storeman.' I asked him when I could start, and he said, 'Now!' At the time I was dressed in sartorial elegance. 'Have you got any work clothes?' he asked. I replied, 'No this is the only suit I've got.' He told me not to worry, they would find me some overalls.

I was taken down to the receiving dock at Elizabeth Street. I was introduced to everyone and they all shouted at me. I said 'You don't have to shout. I understand English.' That's what happens to all new migrants, I suspect. Australians think you don't speak English so they shout, 'How are you?' pronouncing every word clearly. Having established that I could speak the language, they asked where I was from and I said 'I come from Hungary.' 'Hmm,' they said. 'What's the capital of Hungary?' 'Budapest,' I said. All they said was, 'Hmm.' They accepted me anyway, they were lovely, lovely people – ordinary workmen – and in the two years I was to work there I became firm friends with all of them.

That's how I started work. I took my jacket off and put on the overalls they gave me It didn't take much intelligence to catch on to what had to be done. The baskets were enormous and heavy, and they only had two little castors on each side. They came off the truck, up the backlifts and were taken to the appropriate floor. They were hard to push through the carpet. I had to empty all the contents, and then take it down again. Then I got the next basket, and so it went on. By the end of the first day I was almost crying, it was such hard physical work. I was standing in the staff entrance waiting for Eve, leaning against the wall and I actually fell asleep. When Eve came out and found me there she asked me what I had been doing. I said, 'I worked.' And she said, 'Worked? What did you do?' When I said, 'I am a storeman at David Jones,' she shrieked with laughter.

We took the tram back to the guesthouse. We only had a couple of pounds left. We were hungry and so we went into a milkbar and bought a sandwich and a milkshake – that was our dinner. When we arrived at the guesthouse I said, 'I must have a bath.' For each six rooms there was one communal bathroom. We went in and let the water into the tub and got into the bath, the both of us, and the lights failed. It was the time when all the blackouts were happening. Every second day we had blackouts because the electricity services went on strike. And so we sat there in the dark, getting colder in the water. We went into our room which was the size of a toilet; when we walked in we had to get onto the bed in order to close the door. Next morning we went to work again and I walked up to the guy there at the head of the receiving dock at Elizabeth Street and said, 'Look, when do we get paid?' He said, 'You have only just started.' 'Yeah', I said. 'But I don't have any money – period.' He said, 'Well payday's only on Friday.' I told him, 'Look, I don't have money for food.' 'Okay, no worries,' he said, and he loaned me £10.

After my first day as a storeman I knew I wanted to be a musician, and fast. But, to work as a musician in Australia, I learnt, I had to join the Musicians Union. I went and found the union office one lunchtime and went in to apply. The man behind the desk said, 'Oh yeah, no problem at all. Here's the application form.' And so I filled out the form and put it in and asked when I would get an answer. He said, 'Well, actually we'll have a quarterly meeting next week. Come back and I will tell you about it.' Which I did, only to be told that I had been rejected. When I asked why, I was told it was because I was not an Australian citizen. I said 'But you didn't tell me I had to be an Australian citizen to join the union.' 'Oh yes we did,' he replied. I said, 'No, you didn't, otherwise I wouldn't have filled out this application form.' He shrugged. 'Sorry,' he said. 'Well anyhow, when you are an Australian citizen you can join the union.'

Over the course of a year, I applied four times. It became quite farcical. The first time after I had applied for citizenship, I went back to the union and asked if my application could be reconsidered in light of this. 'Sure,' they said. And so I filled out the paperwork again. At the next quarterly meeting – rejected. And so it went on: four times. I'd had a gut full of it; they always left something unsaid. They just wanted to prevent me from joining up, at whatever cost.

I was dejected at first because I thought, 'What the hell am I going to do? I can't be a labourer all my life. I've got better things to do than this.' But then I thought that I could just keep on working and when I became an Australian citizen I could be a musician. But I'd had enough after about a year. I thought, 'No, I'm not going to sit here and waste my life.' My friends at the receiving dock were sympathetic. One of them said, 'Why don't you see the Minister for Immigration?' I said, 'Are you crazy?' 'Go on,' he said. 'Where is he?' I asked. 'Canberra.'

And so one day they covered for me at work. I got on the train in the morning and arrived in Canberra about midday and went straight into the Minister's office. In those days you went into the Minister's and the secretary said, 'What can I do for you?' Not like now. I said, 'I would like to see the Minister.' The secretary said, 'Well, he's in a meeting for about another ten minutes but then you can see him.' The Minister was Harold Holt.

He said, 'Well, tell me a bit about this application form problem.' I told him the whole story and he told me to go back to Sydney, he would take care of it. I got on the train and was back by about six o'clock in the afternoon. Next morning, the headlines in the paper were screaming: 'Musicians Union Disbanded'. And it was – the New South Wales branch was disbanded and deregistered. Then, about three or four days later, it was re-registered with a totally new bunch of people.

Within a week, I got a letter from the Minister saying that my citizenship was being granted; finally, after another trip to Canberra to accept my citizenship papers, I was able to walk into the Musicians Union and say, 'Here is my Australian Citizenship.' It had taken a year and a half. But they still wouldn't have registered me without that Australian Citizenship – rules are rules.

Now I was free to follow my career and I wasted no time. I auditioned for the ABC Radio – this was before television – and they offered me work on a regular broadcast. It was a great feeling, being back in the swing again, but I had another problem. This job alone was not enough to replace my regular work but it was not going to be easy to get the time off for a show during the day. I went to my boss at the receiving dock and I said, 'I've got this radio broadcast on the ABC.' 'What time?' he asked. I told him it was at two o'clock on Thursday and he said, 'You go. We'll cover for you.' Now that was easy to say, but I had to go out through a staff entrance and the guard would ask me where I was going. And so I said, 'I can't do it that way.' My boss told me not to worry.

On the day, one of the truckies came in, and I got into a basket, and was driven out of the building. I climbed out of the basket when we were in the middle of Elizabeth Street and people going by were staring and probably wondering what the hell was going on. The driver said, 'Okay, when will I pick you up?' I told him to come back at quarter to five. And so they smuggled me back in. I did this for about half a year. My workmates were absolutely lovely – I just can't tell you how lovely they were. Of course they heard the broadcast because the radio was on and when I came in they said, 'Oh, that was great. Next time will you play such and such, it's my favourite number.' That I liked!

I kept going back to David Jones for Christmas drinks, years after I had left. They were virtually still the same people there and they were inordinately proud of me. It was lovely. I have never forgotten that warmth and help they gave me. This is why I get so angry and stroppy with people who come here and they believe that they own this place – they don't learn the language, they don't assimilate and I really do hate that.

At that point, at the end of the second year, there was a cut-back on staff, and where both wives and husbands were working, one of them was dismissed. They wanted to dismiss Eve but I said, 'No, no, no! I'm going in her place. She stays!' And so for about two or three months I lived off what she was earning. In the meantime, Gabor in Brisbane formed an ensemble on the local ABC Radio, an eight piece little Palm Court music group. He sent me a letter to say that if I wrote all these special arrangements he would pay me.

I wrote unbelievable amounts of arrangements. That's all I did: I kept writing from seven o'clock in the morning to late at night. I sent him literally hundreds. His group performed them and I got paid. Through this, my name started to be heard on radio – 'Arrangement done by Thomas Tycho'. I kept doing broadcasts but they weren't regular enough – once every two weeks. It payed well but it wasn't enough to live on. Then one day I got a phone call asking me if I would like to work doing duets on two pianos with another pianist. This was a regular weekly job on prime radio time and lasted for six months. The other guy was a fine piano player. I still love him. His name was Glen Marks.

One day, Glen rang me after the six months were over and said, 'Tom, I'm going to New Zealand for a tour.' He had been playing the piano for an ensemble called 'The

Jay Wilbur Strings' and couldn't contact Jay to tell him of his plans. He asked me to take his place for the three months he would be away. I said, 'Well, will you let him know?' 'Yes,' he said. 'I'll ring him. Don't worry, I'll take care of it. You just have to be at the Bourke Street studios in Sydney at a quarter to nine on Tuesday morning.'

So I duly arrived at 8.30a.m. and a kind gentleman with glasses on said, 'What can I do for you?' I said, 'My name is Thomas Tycho.' And he said, 'Yes?' I knew then that Glen hadn't rang. I said to him, 'Well, I've got bad news for you. Glen isn't here and I am taking his place if you'll have me.'

He wasn't entirely happy about the whole situation but he had little choice but to give me a go. 'What was your name again?' he asked. When I told him he said, 'Oh, right, I know who you are. I've heard you on several broadcasts with Glen. Yes, very good. Excellent. Great.' I sat down; the whole orchestra was there. There were about thirty strings. It was lovely, it was beautiful. He said, 'Tommy's now going to take Glen's place. Alright? First number...' and he put it up in front of me. It was a piece called 'The Spinning Song' and I'll never forget it, even today. It was all piano solo, a million notes at the speed of a rocket. I said, 'Okay, here we go,' and Whack! we were into it. Fortunately, I sight - read it without a mistake. The whole orchestra applauded.

Of course it was a test. He wanted to know what I could stand up to, what the standard was. He came over to me and shook my hand and said, 'Great. Okay, you won me.'

Later, I did some orchestration work for him and he was so thrilled he offered me a permanent place in the orchestra. That was more than I had expected and I was uncomfortable at replacing Glen. He said, 'Leave it to me,

I'll fix it.' Indeed he did. He rang Glen in New Zealand and Glen said, 'Look, I was already tired of the broadcast anyhow, so it's great, it's no problem.'

That is what really started my career in this country. And my name was constantly on the ABC as an arranger and piano soloist. The ABC was then The Radio Station. Those were the great days of radio, and I was with them for several years. Soon after that, a couple of years later, the first of the big stadium shows came in.

Lee Gordon was the greatest promoter of overseas talent in this country. The Stadium was the only venue where they could put in 12,000 to 14,000 people. The first big name that Lee Gordon brought in was Johnny Ray. The great Johnny Ray – The Cry Baby. He was the first big American pop star, almost a rock and roller but not quite. He came out and was a huge success. He was here for three weeks. He did nightly shows at the Stadium and on Saturday they had several performances. People were queuing up to see this wonder. He had a big band and it had a very fine piano player. On the last week of Johnny Ray's stay in Australia, on the Friday evening, I got a telephone call from the musical director and he said, 'Tommy, can you do the Johnny Ray show tomorrow at the Stadium?' I was floored. 'Our pianist has taken ill and we need a piano player for tomorrow,' he explained. 'Can you do it?'
Before I knew it, I was there. And so were several thousand screaming people, surrounding the Stadium. I couldn't get through. Finally, I found a side entrance and a cop got me in.

This was no high class venue. It was a smelly stadium and backstage was where all the boxers and the wrestlers usually dressed – it stank to high heaven. There was a guy there and he came up to me and said, 'Aaah, you're Tommy aren't you?' He was Wally Norman, the band leader. He didn't conduct the show because Johnny Ray had brought his own musical director from America, but Wally put the band together. He presented me with a folder, and said, 'Okay, here is the music, have a look at it.'

I flipped right through it – it looked okay, and so I put it back on the table. He looked at me uncertainly and asked, 'Can you do it?' I assured him I could, but judging by the look on his face, I think he was a bit dubious. Wally then introduced me to the musical director. Up until this point, I was quite confident but he then informed me that Johnny Ray was deaf. I said, 'What do you mean he's deaf?' 'He's got a hearing aid.' And I said, 'Oh, great.' But then he said, 'Before each number, you give the key note but really loudly, then he's okay.' I said, 'Alright.' But now I was the one who was dubious.

The moment came and we walked into the stadium ring. The ring was there as it was for the boxing: nothing had changed except that the side rails had been taken off and lights were put on and the orchestra was arranged on the side of it. I walked down on the sloping walkway and suddenly I looked around and thought, 'Oh my God!' There were something like fourteen thousand people. I had never seen so many people in one place in my life. We sat down and played the overture and out came Johnny. He looked down at me in horror, realising it wasn't the same piano man. I looked up and nodded reassuringly, gave him the key note and he smiled. Everything went great. I'm sure I lost at least a kilo in weight at the first concert as I was sweating like a pig. I was sight-reading an entire program which the others had already rehearsed and played for three weeks.

The second concert was much easier and the third one at eight o'clock was a breeze. I was nervous but I was young and cocky and I'd had all that experience already – the experience of someone who was at least thirty years older than I was. It was a gamble but I knew I was going to win it.

I wasn't even thinking of the fact that I wouldn't be able to do it. I just did it.

That one night established me in music in this country more than any other performance. The word spread. 'Hey, did you hear this guy? He just walked straight in and played the show without a rehearsal.' So that's really what pushed my career to a high point. That is how it goes: you first have to win your peers. Once you have won them the rest of it comes easier. The promoters started to hear about it.

After that, the ABC offered me my own ensemble which was palm court-style. It was first called 'The Thomas Tycho Ensemble', and later on, 'The Thomas Tycho Players'. We had regular broadcasts every three weeks or so and made a number of recordings. We played all light, popular music.

For me, at that point, there came a major realisation that I was really doing what I wanted to do. I suddenly saw this as my role in music. I enjoyed light music and I wanted to do it on the highest level possible and make money from it because nobody else did. Classical music has suffered from this unfortunate stigma and it has been there since it started and it probably will be in the future – that you have to be a very big name, an absolute world class name to be able to command any real money from it.

That's just the way it is: you can make a living out of being a good pianist or violinist and so on but it's a mediocre existence; you just live. To make good money from it and make a name for yourself takes a lifetime. Look at the big name stars – people like Pavarotti, or Placido Domingo, or our own Dame Joan. They had to go through blood, sweat and tears before they got there. Even Dame Joan didn't get the name 'La Stupenda' until she was well into her forties. She was always climbing and she was always getting better money and more recordings but by forty-five, almost two thirds of life is gone.

Chapter 6
The Golden Years

The next few years for me were enormously busy. So much so that I almost refused the opportunity to be in at the start of television in Australia. There was a band leader by the name of Les Welsh who was a very well known jazz singer/piano player/band leader, and he got the job of putting together a small band of about eight or nine players. Les was a limited pianist and he needed somebody in the band who could play the whole spectrum – accompanying singers doing jazz, solos, whatever. He said to me on one of these sessions on radio, 'Would you like to do television?' I said, 'Oh, I don't know I'm so busy.' He said, 'Well I believe this show called 'Sydney Tonight' will start as soon as Channel Seven starts and it will be a nightly live show.' And he asked me to join.

Television started in Australia with Channel Nine in about September of 1956. Channel Seven started in December of that year. At first, very few people could afford it: it would have been an ordinary person's three month salary to buy one. I can recall hundreds of people standing in front of the electrical shops at night, standing there as long as the transmission was on, watching and listening to the programs on the televisions in the windows.

I remember that Eve and I were living in Mosman at the time, and we went up to the main street like everybody else and watched this incredible, marvellous event, the first TV transmission. We were all conscious of a new age starting, aware of the fact that here was a situation where, in a studio somewhere in Sydney somebody was looking into a camera reading the news and several miles away we could see that same thing happening. Until then, talking over the telephone was a natural thing. But to see a person's face at the same time, it was a new age. Today, if you could see it you would laugh your head off, it was so juvenile. But it was the start of an era which hasn't finished yet.

At Channel Seven, we rehearsed in a half-finished building, and then came the opening night. We were there from morning in the closed studio and we didn't know what was happening outside. It was pouring with rain and the area wasn't concreted with a walkway – it was red mud. All the VIPs, including the Prime Minister, arrived in limousines, and stepped out and squelched in the red mud. It was hysterical. People were coming in with their socks and their shoes, ladies in high heeled shoes, covered with red mud! Anyhow, the opening went ahead; it was a Sunday, and from then on there was no looking back.

On Monday night the show started live on air and it was on for two years. It was unbelievable. There was new material every night. It was a show like 'The Tonight Show' -- a program of interviews and musical items. The host was Keith Walsh from Adelaide. He was a radio personality on 2GB in those days. He was a kind of comic as well. It was a nightly show broadcast every week night. At that time there were no live shows on Saturday or Sunday. It had what is called a 'home set', which meant it was looking through a window with a big picture of Sydney at night in the background. In front of the window, facing the camera, was a big desk and behind the desk the presenter was sitting, interviewing people and introducing performers. That was the format. As well as the home set there was an orchestral set and a main area where the artists would appear.

'The Sydney Tonight Show' proved to be enormously successful. All of a sudden the management saw there was something really good happening, and to capitalise on it they decided to add a variety show on Saturday night. This meant that we had to prepare yet another program, and one that was more sophisticated and more organised. It was an hour-long variety program which included dancers, jugglers, singers and other performers. We started rehearsing at ten o'clock on Saturday morning and continued until six, then had an hour for dinner. At eight o'clock the show was on. Arrangements had to be written and there was a lot of work involved in scheduling and in planning which artists would appear when. That show proved to be very successful too; then some bright spark realised there was no live show on Sunday. And so they said, 'Now we are going to add something else!'

This was a classical program performed live on Sunday; it was sponsored by the Commonwealth Bank. It was called 'The Commonwealth Bank Hour of Music'. It was a different style of music from the variety shows but with the same band, same orchestra – musicians are versatile.

Those first few years were manic. It was sheer madness, the hours we worked, sometimes up to 120 hours a week. I lived at Channel Seven. In the beginning, it was incredibly exciting and it shaped and formed the person I am. Eventually though, it went beyond exciting, it became too much. It was very intense. Each performance was a one-off, so it was, in effect, a premiere. It was like being catapulted into a situation that I couldn't get away from even if I wanted to. There was a momentum to it and it kept on going at this million-mile-an-hour-pace all the time. It meant that there was no room for ruminating or to deliberate on things: you made decisions instantly and that was it.

As things progressed, I gathered more staff around me. There were about four, five or six orchestrators who helped me – I didn't do it all. But as well as that, there were meetings, planning of programs, practising, rehearsing, and arranging to be done. It was a way of life. I hardly saw my family. By 1961 things became more organised and the pace less frantic. But the first four years of television from 1956 to 1960 were absolute madness. All my time and energy was just totally absorbed by Channel Seven.

There were many people who were outstanding in that whole experience. It was one of the truly great pleasures of the time to be working with creative people on such a high level. We were all on the same wave-length. For instance, one of the greatest jazz pianists in this country, Julian Lee the blind pianist, who was originally from New Zealand, was one of my musical arrangers. Can you imagine that? He was writing his orchestrations in braille, then he taped it and somebody transcribed it from the tape recorder into music score. He still does that. He is brilliant, absolutely brilliant. The process sounds complicated, but strangely enough it doesn't take much longer than if I sat down and started to write an orchestration. It could probably take another one third as long because of the dictation.

In every situation there is always going to be somebody who's uncooperative, and naturally we had some frictions. But I cannot remember any that stand out. I can honestly say it was a glorious time, with everybody pitching in to do the best they could, and we were proud of the shows we did. Everybody pushed themselves beyond their capabilities to make things better and if we had to work until two o'clock in the morning, we worked until two o'clock in the morning. We may have been falling over with exhaustion, but we did it.

I was always open and friendly, and I spoke to anybody. I got upset like everybody else but I was just a human being who happened to be in the pit of all this madness. I was involved in not only the music part of it, but also the choreography. The choreographer would come to me and say, 'Four weeks from now I want to do so and so. How do we do it?' or 'Do you think I should do it?' Then we would have to work out the staging and formats and so on.

It was a ridiculous way to live but I was paid very well. By the late 1950's, I was earning well in excess of £150 a week, which was big money. At first we lived in Mosman in a little apartment and then we saw a house in Seaforth and we bought it for £6,500. It was the same style of cottage we could have bought for £500 when we first arrived here. By that time it was £6,500. It was a nice home. We were only the two of us then; Vicky was born in 1959 and later my mother came out from Hungary, and it proved to be too small. We bought our next house in Seaforth, not very far away from there, and it seemed like a palace.

I was pleased that mother eventually came out to Australia to live. I would have loved my sister to settle here too. She has been out to visit at least four times in the last fourteen years or so, but because she was married, she didn't want to stay here. This is the rather tragic dilemma of a lot of people who lived behind the Iron Curtain. In order for her to be able to come out, she had to leave her husband there and that was the hardest part. The first time she came, she was here for about six months and both Eve and my mother, who was already here, begged her, 'Stay here; we will get him out somehow.' But she wouldn't risk it in case he couldn't get out. And so she went back. Some years later I got her out again and it was the same story all over again: she went back because her husband was there. Then our mother passed away and we brought my sister out again, but by this time she was too old and, as the saying goes, you cannot transplant an old tree. She speaks English fluently, probably better than most of the migrants who live here, so she would have had no problem fitting in. But we didn't even approach that subject any more because I thought, 'What's the use?' She has lived most of her life in Budapest, she has her friends and family there; it is her environment and she would not be happy away from it.

Meanwhile, my life at Channel Seven was going along at a hectic pace. A lot of performers came on to the show night after night, and I was the one who had to accompany them. The rehearsals usually started at 7.30p.m. in a little shack outside the main building which, in the early days, wasn't completed. Normally, all the musical content was rehearsed and so there was no problem. My first experience of total terror was very early on. One night, one of the artists who was supposed to arrive didn't turn up. The producer, Frank Strain, rushed down during one of the commercial breaks and yelled at me, 'We want you to play a piano solo after the next commercial break. We've got somebody who is to be interviewed, which will last fifteen minutes and then we go to a commercial break. Keith will announce that you'll be playing a piano solo.' It wasn't a matter of asking, 'Have you got anything that you can play?' It was, 'Tom, you are going to play.'

During the commercial break the stagehands wheeled

the piano away from the band to centre stage, put the mike in and I played a couple of passages to get the sound. After the commercial break Keith said, 'Our band leader pianist is now going to play a piano solo called, 'The Dream of Olwyn.' I remember that much! Then I started to play and the next few minutes are a total black-out, blotted out of my memory forever. I presume I played it and I played it well, because the next thing I remember was the applause of the studio audience. I still can't remember how I did it, or what I did: I was only told that it was fine. That experience was, for me, sheer terror, and it's the only time I can recall that happening to me. I can't remember stage fright on concert platforms or in radio – naturally, you get tight in the chest, the adrenalin starts pumping – if it didn't you wouldn't be the artist that you are – but that's a natural thing, you get keyed up for the performance. I suppose a lot of performers experience something similar to my terror the very first time they perform.

The early days of television were something – absolutely magical. The anecdotes would be enough to fill another book. Those things are not captured any more, that spontaneity, because the spirit, the novelty the excitement were unique and because all of us were learning on the job.

Anybody who came visiting Australia was grabbed to appear on 'The Sydney Tonight Show' along with local people – anyone who had an interesting story to tell. There was one incident that sticks in my mind. Johnny Mathis came in to do one of the Stadium shows, like Johnny Ray, and of course he was dragged into the studio before he did the concerts: so that people would know he was here and would go to the concerts and also because he was a big name. He was ushered in to be interviewed by Keith Walsh.

Somebody had the idea that it would be nice to present a wallaby to this great person, not realising that he was totally afraid, petrified, of animals. At the end of the interview one of the stage hands brought this charming little wallaby out and plonked it onto the desk in front of Johnny Mathis. Of course, animals get frightened the moment they are out of their own environment and can do all kinds of funny things. This one started peeing, and kept on peeing and peeing, and it flooded the desk and flowed over the side.

In the meantime, nobody noticed the fact that Johnny stood up very quietly and backed away until he was leaning against the set. He was absolutely petrified out of his wits looking at this animal. If it were a cat or a dog it might have been alright, but this was a small kangaroo and he had never seen anything like it in his life. He was standing there, nailed to the wall. The live audience were literally rolling on the floor in agony, just about peeing themselves. The orchestra was beside itself: we were falling out of our chairs. When the wallaby first started peeing, Keith sort of said, 'Oh... Aaah,' and then he saw that the camera was panning down. He had the monitor and could see that it was going to air. He just said, 'There he is. Umm... well... He's really disgracing himself.' And he kept on talking about the wallaby.

By this time, the audience was in hysterics and so were the crew in the studio and the orchestra, and nobody was taking any notice of Johnny Mathis, until suddenly one of the cameras caught him and went straight onto him. He was just standing there, frozen with fear. It lasted for what seemed like five minutes until the director cut to a commercial break. They couldn't get Johnny Mathis off the wall until they took the wallaby away. He was still standing there – he was in shock.

There were no video tapes in those days so it isn't on tape today but it would be hysterical to see it again. It was one of those things that only happen on live television; a classic. I wish they would do it like that nowadays because they would get all these kinds of things happening. Today they keep editing everything so that it becomes antiseptic.

There was another incident I recall. I had to play another solo and we were, by now, real veterans of television because we had done several hundred shows, and productions had started to become a little bit more sophisticated. The band had been expanded into a twelve piece band and I was quite used to doing piano solos.

On this occasion, the producer and director had the great idea of having me on camera playing the piano and having another camera separately focussed on a real fire which would be lit in the studio. They would then matt the two together so that in the final shot I would appear to be sitting in the centre of a fire ring playing my piece, 'The Ritual Fire Dance'. In order to achieve this, a piece of very thick rope was first submerged in kerosene then put into a metal plate to be lit at a particular signal. Everything was live. There were no videos, it had to be done live. They were experimental times. And so when the time came we went into a commercial, and the producer ran down and said to one of the stage hands, 'Okay, now you light the fire.' And so he lit the rope, which started to emit some flames. By the time I started playing, the flames were about four feet high. The rope was full of kerosene and it started burning and kept on burning. Eventually, the flames leapt about twenty feet into the studio! I was totally unaware of it because I was playing the piano some distance away from all this. It looked like the studio itself was going to catch on fire. This was live on air. The audience, by this time, was halfway out of their seats, ready to escape at a moment's notice, and I still kept on playing. All of a sudden I saw all this commotion out of the corner of my eye; I could see that there was a total disaster happening but I had to keep on playing the damn thing. I finished it and by that time the fire engines were coming because somebody rang the fire department. They dowsed the flames. It was absolutely hysterical.

There was another marvellous one – the first Christmas show that we did. The orchestra was on set right throughout the show and at one point a soloist was supposed to sing one of the Christmas songs, starting at the back of the set facing the camera and slowly walking towards it. It was staged so that, as she walked, the camera would keep the orchestra in the background and eventually she would end up at the front of the stage with the orchestra far in the background and virtually out of focus.

On either side, as she was walking, there was a row of columns. The problem, of course, was that in those days there were no lapel microphones. All the sound recording was done on the boom. To be able to do that, they had to have two boom microphones on wheels and they were tracked close to the singer's mouth, out of camera range. In order to get the sound and not lose the voice at all, one boom microphone was going from column to column on the left hand side and the other was ready to pick up the signal from the columns on the right side. In theory, it seemed alright, but it wasn't rehearsed because there was no time. What happened was this: the young boom operators, who had to winch in the boom and winch it out again in order to go past each column, were a bit nervous. The very first boom, as the operator was racking it in, just hit the column ever so slightly – they were not real columns at all, they were papier-maché – and this thing toppled right in front of the singer. In typical show-business tradition she just stepped over it. By this time the other boom was about to pick her up and that guy, seeing this mishap, was also very nervous and mis-timed himself and hit the next column. Needless to say, the sixteen columns, one after the other, kept on falling in front of the singer. It looked like the most carefully rehearsed comedy sketch you had ever seen. There was this poor woman singing a religious Christmas song and the audience was roaring with laughter because they thought it was a comedy segment.

I think that particular program was jinxed, because another disaster occurred. The orchestra had a fascia in front of them to cover up the untidy sight of music stands, – everything had to look pretty. However, it was summertime, this being Christmas, and the poor band was roasting and they said, 'Look, how about we just put on our jackets with shorts and thongs because we won't be seen?' The producer reluctantly agreed to it because it was stinking hot in the studio. But, of course, what happened? We started playing a number and somebody accidentally kicked the fascia and it toppled over. There was the entire orchestra in jackets, shorts, and thongs in full view of the audience. The audience and studio crew were absolutely in hysterics because they thought it was all planned. But it wasn't – it was supposed to be a very religious Christmas show. If you planned it as a comedy show you couldn't have done it any better. Of course, Keith came back and said, 'Well, I hope you enjoyed that because we really meant to do it– we really wanted you to laugh.' It was an absolute untruth, in those days you had to think on your feet. After that incident the memos went flying: 'The orchestra must, at all times, be fully dressed, with black socks and black shoes.'

Another time, I remember, there was a special South American theme night, and the set designers and the producers started to get very adventurous. The orchestra was built up into an inverted shape like a pyramid. At the top of it, at the pinnacle, sat drummer, Tommy Spencer. Behind him was a big set all done out in South American motifs. It looked grand because the camera could pan up and down and sideways across the band. But, of course, what happened? As always, though the plans were perfectly laid, something went amiss.

We started playing. It was a really throbbing South American samba and the set began to tremble behind us because of the volume and the pulse of the music. It was all made from flimsy wood and material, and one of the nails worked loose. Then another nail worked loose and slowly the whole set started to bend towards the drummer and eventually it fell on his head. At first, the rest of us didn't even notice. We weren't aware of Tommy's plight but gradually the set engulfed more and more of us and finally, the whole orchestra was covered by it. This was all on camera and they didn't stop until we stopped the music. When the number finished, again the audience was in total hysteria because they thought this was planned. You couldn't plan anything like that in a million years.

There were so many things that could go wrong and did go wrong. There was one particular occasion when I had to accompany an opera singer and she was totally petrified. She started singing but forgot the middle section of the song. I heard her stop at the end of the first phrase, and suddenly she started singing the beginning and so I went back to the beginning with her. When we came to the middle section again, I could see by her glassy eyes that she had a mental block but this time I was prepared and when she went back to the beginning of it again I jumped with her. We kept on playing these eight bars for about a minute and a half until suddenly the producer realised what was happening and went to a commercial break in the middle of it. It was like a record that was stuck in a groove. I had visions of playing the same thing over and over forever. The poor woman burst into tears and she must have been totally devastated by it, but these things happened. That is what makes experience and that's what makes a presence of mind – thinking on your feet and trying to save the day.

Not all the problems were technical failings. There was often a lively sense of mischief at play too. On one occasion, early in the 'Sydney Tonight' days, it was the first time that Slim Dusty sang the song 'Pub With No Beer', which had been a recent hit. We were doing a big production of it. I was with the band on the main set and Slim and his band were in front of us, and to introduce some comedy into it they put a fake tap on the side of the piano. Everyone was to have a glass of beer with them and at the end of the number, before they went to black, everyone was to raise their glass and drink.

This was fine, except my drink was laced. I leant towards the tap, made out I was filling my glass from it, then raised it, drank it down and almost in the same movement threw it up again. It was soap. It was a very bad joke! I never did find out exactly who was responsible but a lot of people looked very sheepish.

There was no link between Sydney and Melbourne in the beginning. Occasionally, shows were sent down, but it was only during the Olympics that there was a kind of relay mechanism on top of hills, linking the country. That was in 1956. This link was only for that particular occasion, so that the Sydney group could also see what happened in Melbourne. By the third year of television, they had the first proper link through the relay stations on top of hills so they could send programs from Melbourne to Sydney and vice versa. In general, production started to become more slick and by the time we came to 1960 it was very good television. I still feel that the golden years of television were from 1960 to 1968 or 1970. Then it just went into decline, and I feel that television today is not what it is supposed to be. The live content has been taken out. When they make a mistake they simply stop and say, 'Okay, take two'. Everything is videoed and edited and they lose the spontaneity of things happening, which to me, added the excitement, the essence of television.

Chapter 7
Opportunities

In 1961 Channel Seven started a magnificent series of musical programs. By this time they had a thirty-six piece orchestra, a twenty piece choir, a sixteen piece chorus line with dancers, and a ballet core of about eight, with three choreographers. It was backed by totally sophisticated machinery to create high class music shows of international standard which were shown every Sunday night between seven-thirty and eight-thirty. Australia virtually stopped to watch these programs. Everything stopped. There were people who wouldn't even go out to the loo while they were watching this. The shows featured world class names. They were big sophisticated productions.

Through these television specials marvellous opportunities opened for me. If a promoter wanted to bring a big name performer out to Australia – and in those days it was done in conjunction with one or another of the television stations – as soon as the contract was signed, I was approached by the performer's organisation to conduct the orchestra in the pit for the tour.

This is what happened when Jack Benny came out. At the time, Jack was at the pinnacle of his television career and his shows were shown in Australia, and the tickets just went in five minutes. I was thrilled to be associated with a world star like Jack. When he arrived, I got a telephone call from his manager, saying that he would like to meet me at his hotel. When I arrived I was directed up to the top floor to the executive suite. I knocked on the door and heard a voice from the other side: 'Come in.' I opened the door and walked in, and there in middle of the suite, was Jack Benny standing in his underpants, smoking a big Havana cigar. He looked at me and said, 'Yes?' I said, 'Mr Benny, my name is Tommy Tycho.' And he said, 'Ah, come in dear boy.'

Jack was a gentle and very charming, articulate person. I had a great time with him and I learnt from my association with him that with stars, the greater they are, the more gentle, the more approachable, the more beautiful they are. We spent one week in rehearsals. This was followed by two weeks that were a total sell-out here in Sydney, and two weeks in Melbourne.

His show was a classic, quality show: not a four letter word was ever spoken. He didn't need to; it was genuinely funny and he could tell such stories. He also made a point of introducing new artists from Australia. One whose career he helped was Johnny O'Keefe, who was a young, up and coming star but not yet the big teenage idol he would become.

Jack Benny had one routine which I always enjoyed. Towards the end of the show he would talk about the fact that he really was a violinist and he would egg the audience on. 'Would you like me to play the violin?' He would ask. he did this in a way that suggested he was an awful violinist. In fact, he played the violin well – to play that badly you have to be a good musician! But he was a frustrated one. The audience, of course, started laughing and clapping and then he looked into the wings and said, 'May I have my violin please?' And he kept talking. Half a minute or so later he looked into the wings again and said, 'Excuse me, but could I have my violin please?' He kept looking with that famous look of his, and eventually out flew a violin from the wings to end up at his feet, broken into a million pieces – it was a breakable violin made especially for the act. The audience was roaring with laughter and Jack looked at them and said, 'OK, fine.' Then he said, 'Now, may I have my violin please?' and it was brought out to him. As he was tuning the violin a little girl yelled from the audience, 'I can do that,' and he looked down and said, 'Oh really? You can do that?' 'Yeah,' she called back, 'I'm a violinist.'

'Well, will you come up here please?' he said and then he asked if she could play a certain piece and he played a phrase on the violin. She grabbed the violin out of his hands and played a huge cadenza and he just stood by, looking. 'You can now go back to your seat!' It was all set up – this young violinist actually toured with him. It was a gentle kind of humour which was really genuine, and it reflected the kind of man he was.

There was only one time he failed to charm. It was when we went to Melbourne, just after the Westgate Bridge collapsed. He did the routine, the violin flew out and landed at his feet and as he picked it up, all broken and held together only by the strings, he delivered the line, 'The bridge is broken just like yours.' And there was a total silence. He looked down at me in the pit, horrified that there was no reaction. When the show was over he came to me and asked, 'What's wrong with these people in Melbourne?' I said, 'Well, I think this is just so tragic to them.' And so he never mentioned it again. He just didn't expect it to be taken to heart like that. I know that people were hurt and some died in that tragedy but I think it was a funny line and maybe we were just a little too parochial to joke about it.

One day, Jack said to me, 'What are you doing on Sunday?' I said, 'Nothing, in particular. Why?' He said,

'Well, I really would like to play the violin with you.' We were staying at a hotel and he said, 'I'll book the ballroom, so we'll have it all afternoon, because I'd like us to play good music together.' He said, 'You invite Eve so she can be the audience.' We had lunch and went into the ballroom and we played for at least four or five hours, with Eve sitting by herself knitting and listening to this unrehearsed concert. He enjoyed it immensely because he always wanted to be a good violinist. He wasn't a bad one either. He started out as a musician in the pit. Because he wanted to make more money, eventually he developed an act as a violinist but when he played the violin he was bombarded with onions and rotten food because people wanted to see something more than just a man standing up there playing the violin. Then somebody eventually said, 'Why don't you tell some funny stories?' And so he kept playing the violin and interrupting himself and telling funny stories and he became a big hit. This was a long time ago, back in the old vaudeville days which was long before television, but that's how his act came about.

He was a lovely, gentle person and we just clicked, even though he was much older than I was. In fact we celebrated his seventieth birthday during those concerts in Sydney. There was one occasion when Eve and I were having dinner with him. Eve, being a great movie buff, was plaguing him with questions. She asked him what his favourite movie was and he said it was a film called, 'To Be Or Not To Be' which was directed by a friend of his, a famous Hollywood director, the Hungarian born Ernst Lubitsch. Like Jack himself, this man had never said a bad word in his life. Jack would even hesitate when he said 'damn'. He proceeded to relate this story about how, while making this film, he and Ernst went out to lunch. He recounted: 'Ernst all of a sudden looked at me and said,

"Jack, wouldn't it be nice to have two penises?" I had never ever heard him say such a thing. I said, "Excuse me, but what did you say?" So he repeated it. "Wouldn't it be nice to have two penises?" I was totally stunned. "Whatever for?" I asked. Ernst said, "Well, one of your own and a good one as well."'

That joke coming out of the mouth of a man who had never said anything like that, had such an impact that we nearly fell off our chairs. He was really quite exceptional. That was the way he was, and that was how he timed his comedy on stage. He was full of surprises and full of fun, in his private life as much as on stage. He delivered his lines in a sort of gentle, very underplayed way. I'll remember that as long as I live. He had diabetes and he was not supposed to eat sweets or smoke but he had these huge, big Havana cigars which never came out of his mouth. It wasn't just a prop, he was smoking. He smoked about six or seven a day – that was his great joy.

If Jack Benny was one of the nicest people I met, one of the least pleasant was certainly Frank Sinatra. I could appreciate the fact that the man resented being hounded by the press most of the time. But because of the kind of high profile person that he was, the antics that he got up to, and all the things that happened to him, I could also understand why he was hounded. I used to say, with sincerity, that I really felt sorry for him until I met him. Then I changed my mind. I think he was really a horrible person, one of the few people I have met who was simply not a nice human being.

Having said that though, I admire him immensely as an artist. To me, he is the epitome of pop singing. He established the format, the way in which people today sing pop songs. He put so much into a song; you could understand every word he said, and he made a banal set of lyrics sound like a poem. The way he treated the songs, the way he delivered the passion, the romance, the drama, everything – it was like a three act play to hear a three minute song from Sinatra. He was the one who started it, he struck the pattern which is still followed the world over.

Before him there were lots of good pop singers but none of them had the incredible charisma and approach to songs that he had. Mind you, he was choosey: he didn't sing just any song. He chose the ones he could do something with and he put his own style and character into them. As far as that was concerned, as an artist, he was one of the greatest, in my opinion, and he was a very credible actor too. Along side him, another great singer Bing Crosby was very laid back. Bing had great style for singing romantic ballads but Sinatra was a jazz singer.

As a human being though I thought he was rotten. The first and only time I was associated with him on the same stage was when he came over to do his second or third visit: he had been a frequent visitor, coming every three or four years to do a tour. On this particular occasion I had the great fortune of making a television special with Stan Freeberg, a very witty and funny man. He was the support act for Sinatra and asked me to be his musical director. He would start the show off with his comedy routine, then Sinatra would come on.

When we got to Melbourne, where the tour started, we found that the venue was Festival Hall, a big stadium used for all kinds of events like boxing and wrestling. It was the only place large enough to stage Sinatra. It had no private dressing rooms, just one giant communal dressing room for all the sportsman to use. Stan and I were on one side of this room and across the other side, about fifteen metres away, was Sinatra. At that time Ava Gardner was filming 'On The Beach' in Melbourne. I think that was one of the reasons he came out to Australia, and he timed his tour to coincide with her being here because he was head over heels in love with her

As we were the show-starters we were always at the Hall before him. While we were getting prepared to go down into the arena and do the performance, Sinatra and his minders arrived. They were on the other side of the dressing room. Sinatra glared at us, because he didn't want us there. One of his minders, a character with a broken nose and flat ears, came over and said, 'He wants you out of here.'

Now Stan was a big hit. He had a huge name in America and in the world as the greatest comic in the world. Stan said, 'You can tell him that we'll go when we're ready.' This guy just stood there because he couldn't do anything except repeat, 'The Pope wants you out of here.' Stan just walked straight up to him and said, 'You go back and tell the Pope that we'll go when we're ready,' Sinatra was the boss of the rat pack. He was often called the Pope, the Emperor or the Chairman. The guy couldn't do anything, he just turned around and went back and told Sinatra that we were not moving. Then they moved, they left the place. They went back to the hotel. There was this kind of expectation: 'Sinatra's come in, so everybody out!' I mean who the hell was he apart from being a very great artist? The whole concept of calling him a name as if he ruled the world – it was a joke!

That's just one tiny incident which gives you an insight into the man's thinking and his self-importance and the conceit that he had. He would walk surrounded by about six bodyguards, all of them Mafia types. As soon as he arrived somewhere it was: 'Okay, tell all these nobodies to leave.' Every night though, I always waited to listen to him when he was on stage because on stage it was a different kettle of fish. It was a duality which I suppose came from his very disturbing and bad childhood. He was virtually a street kid who had had to fight his way through.

Towards the end of my time at Channel Seven, I spent one of the craziest years of my life working two jobs. I was still Musical Director at Channel Seven and was doing a couple of nightly shows, including the 'Bob Rogers Tonight Show' twice a week. At the time, the Chevron Hotel in Sydney had one of the two biggest nightclubs in the country. It was called 'The Silver Spade' and it was big. In its day, it was the place: all the big acts played there. There was another one called 'Chequers Nightclub'. The two competed against each other, bringing out the biggest names that they could find. The Chevron has since been pulled down and today, there is a big Japanese hotel there called the Nikko. But it still has a bar called 'The Silver Spade' in honour of the club

There was a kind of association between the Chevron and Channel Seven, and the acts which performed at the Silver Spade also appeared on Channel Seven. At this time, there had been some problem with the previous musical director at the Silver Spade and so they approached Channel Seven and asked if they could use me to be their musical director as well.

The Chevron had a dinner show at seven-thirty and a night time show at 11.00p.m. six nights a week. That was fine except for when I was doing the Tonight Show as well, because this was sandwiched in between the dinner show and the night time show at the Silver Spade. I often spent those evenings driving at high speed between the Chevron and Channel Seven to cover all three shows. It was madness, but when I accepted it I didn't even think about it – it just seemed to be an incredibly exciting challenge Eve kept saying, 'You're kidding yourself.' I said, 'No, it's okay. It's okay.' It wasn't of course. It was insane to work at such a pace but it was many years before I came to realise that.

The shows themselves were enough work, but I also had to rehearse. I would rehearse for one show in the morning and another show in the afternoon. It meant I went from Seaforth, where I lived, to Channel Seven to rehearse with the artists of that night's Tonight Show and then I would drive into the city, do another rehearsal, get the dinner suit on, and do the first show at the nightclub. The shows at the Silver Spade were big floor shows with a fairly large orchestra, and you had to be really on the ball because they were in front of a live audience. As soon as the dinner show was finished I would race out to the waiting limousine and be driven at high speed to get to Channel Seven twenty minutes before the Tonight Show was due to start. Then, with barely a moment to mop my brow, I was driven back to the Chevron for the eleven o'clock night show. It was madness. They were ten and twelve hour days, and for all that time I had to be fully on the ball. It was stupid but it was also very exciting.

In the heyday of the Silver Spade I worked with a number of amazing people: Mel Torme the great jazz singer, he was called 'the Velvet Fog', and Roy Orbison was another one. He was a big star by then with lots of hits, but he was still not comfortable on stage. On the first night that he played, he got out in front of the audience with his dark glasses and guitar. He planted his two feet in front of the orchestra and sang for an hour. He didn't say a word. Not even 'Good evening, ladies and gentlemen' or 'Thankyou'. He just sang one song after another.

Now, he had his father touring with him, a lovely man, and after the show his father and I were talking. He asked me what I thought of the show and I said, 'He should have spoken to the audience, welcomed them'. 'Good idea' he said, and the next show, Roy came out and said, 'Good evening ladies and gentlemen,' and at the end of the show he said, 'Thankyou very much for your attendance.' And that was it. In between, he still just stood and sang one song after another.

After this show, his dad said to me, 'Well, how was that?' I said, 'Great, but how about a bit more? Get him to introduce some of the numbers.' For the third show, Roy said, 'Good evening,' then announced the title of every song, and at the end said, 'Thankyou'. His dad came to me after that one, with a big beaming smile. 'So, was that good?' he asked. 'No,' I said. 'You have to tell him to communicate, to talk to the audience. Say anything, tell jokes, anecdotes.' Roy began to talk more and finally, after the three week season, he was doing it. And so I like to think that I was, in some small way, helpful in teaching him something of his stage craft.

Before the madness of that year began, I had already been thinking that it was almost time to move on. I had that feeling again, that I was only treading water, doing television shows that I'd done for the past twelve to fourteen years. There didn't seem to be anything new or challenging. I can see now that the main reason I accepted the job at the Silver Spade was because I wanted the sense of excitement and challenge.

I was glad that I did it, because in that time I was associated with some great performers. For years the big name artists used to bring all their key musical people with them – their musical directors, pianists, drummers, bass player, lead trumpet, saxophonist, trombonist – because they didn't know what they were going to get here and they wanted to ensure that their standard of performance would not suffer.

By the time Mel Torme came out he was on his own, which is a great credit to all of us in Australia because we were acknowledged as having lifted our game to the international standard. It was particularly pleasing for me because, in my case, he didn't bring his own musical director. At the time, I didn't realise how much of a compliment it was. I realise it now but then I just thought, 'Oh, he came by himself. Okay, well I will conduct the show.' You know, you don't rationalise things like that until many many years afterwards. He came out and we became friends within the first minute. He had an incredibly entertaining program. It was one of the greatest musical treats for me to work with such a talented, creative man like that.

When Judy Garland did her cabaret act for a world tour, he set it up for her. He set up acts for big name artists, like Judy, and Robert Goulet. He would work with them to establish what items they should sing and how they should sing them. That is what I have done since with artists in Australia – people like Julie Anthony, Anthony Warlow and Jackie Love. I learnt a lot from Mel Torme.

One other gentleman whom I enjoyed working with very much was Henry Mancini. That was an eye-opener. Again, he was the most gentle, the most intelligent, articulate person you could ever meet. When we went down to breakfast at seven o'clock he looked the epitome of sartorial elegance. He always looked like he just came out of one of those exclusive shops. He wore a fresh tie and fresh shirt, every time I saw him.

To work with the calibre of musicians like Henry Mancini probably lifted my game without my realising it. In the beginning I was daunted by them because these were names I had seen on the screen and television, and all of a sudden I thought, 'Holy mackerel, I'm working with this person!' I learned an enormous amount. I was a very astute observer. I was overawed by their talent, by their sleekness, by their sophistication, by their whole behaviour on stage in front of an audience. Automatically, I emulated them without even rationalising what I was learning, without consciously thinking, 'That was done by Jack Benny'. I just absorbed things.

It was not always easy because these people were demanding, very demanding. They had to have everything perfect every time. I learned one thing from them: when people come to see you, they pay their money and sometimes the money is very big money and they want the perfect performance. They are not interested in the fact that your mother just died a couple of minutes ago, or that you've got a toothache, or you've got your period – they are not interested in all that. They come in, they want to be entertained and that's it. That's what I have learned from all these big name artists. Every performance has got to be a 110 per cent, not 100 per cent and that's the way it is.

Ethel Mermann was an absolute delight to work with. She was a gorgeous girl who wanted everything just so. Even in rehearsal she would stop and say, 'No, that's not right. Let's do it again.' She would do this until it was absolutely perfect. Then she would say, 'Now, that's the way I want it done every performance.' She was at the Silver Spade for three weeks, which meant an evening show and a night time show and so all up, we did about forty to fifty performances, and every performance had to be a 110 per cent. It wasn't a holiday but if you delivered the goods the stars were as gorgeous and charming and friendly as anyone. If you didn't — then you were out on your ear in five minutes and they would get somebody else who was capable of it.

I had to automatically, uncompromisingly match their standard once I had matched that, I could not allow myself to perform below that for any reason whatsoever. I keet on saying that I would love to be a perfectionist because there is no such thing as a perfect performance and there never can be. There's always something creeping in, a little blemish, but trying to eliminate all those things was what I was always trying to do. People might say they are perfectionists but I don't agree: they cannot be, they just want to be perfectionists and they want to be as good as it is absolutely humanly possible to be. That's my own drive. I wasn't aware of it for two decades. I just did things and always kept on doing them better and better. I drove everybody around me to do it better, not by being nasty but just by saying, 'No, no, let's do this again. It's not right.' They'd say, 'No, it's okay.' But I'd say, 'No, no it's not. Let's do it again.' I was urging everybody around me all the time – musicians, artists – until it was really right. Then I thought 'Aaah, now this is good.' I was satisfied. Probably, till the end of my days, my motivation will be the same. I want to provide the top class ultimate in performance in every case when I'm facing an audience.

Jerry Lewis was also at the Silver Spade. He was there for two weeks, and we became firm friends. I find that happens when I have to associate with people for a short space of time and it's an intense relationship. They may forget about me two years later, and when my name comes up they might say, 'Oh yeah, I remember something,' but during that period of time it's an intense relationship – because of my drive for making it as perfect as possible, because of the reputation they have to maintain and sustain at a high level. Jerry wanted everything so perfect that it was painful. But at the beginning before the first show, he said, 'Tommy, you have to be 200 per cent because then, when you ease off, you still do 100 per cent.' And I agree with him.

One night, after an evening show, we were going out. I accompanied him back to his suite while he got changed. As he started to shed his clothes he said, 'Look at me. It's like I've been standing in a shower. I'm dripping wet.' I said, 'Jerry, you've just done an hour and forty-five minute show; of course you are wet.' He said 'No, no, no! It's because I was struggling in the first thirty minutes to get going.' I said, 'Well, you could have fooled me. I thought you were terribly funny, as always.' He said, 'No, no I'll prove it to you.' The next show he did was absolutely sensational; people were roaring with laughter and he received a standing ovation. At the end of it, as he went back to the dressing room he called, 'Tommy, come out with me.' He showed me his clothes and they were absolutely dry this time, and he said, 'You see, I didn't have to fight.'

It was a lesson I have always remembered.

I can relate an interesting aside; Jerry came for about two weeks, which included about fifty-four performances, and he bought fifty-four identical dinner suits, shirts, ties, socks and shoes. He never wore the same one after a performance. It was one of those quirks. Then he had it all packed by his valet into a huge trunk and shipped back to America, to be drycleaned.

I was lucky to have been given these insights into the workings of top international stars. How do you think they got to the top? Not because they were flukes. There are those flukes who last a moment and then disappear into nothing but with these people, the ones I have mentioned, they got to the top because they had the drive, and the talent and experience. They don't always have an extra special talent, but the ones who stay are the ones who have been able to capitalise on what they have. With these people talent is a forgone conclusion: without it they have no hope in the world, but talent has to be developed, nurtured and made into something bigger than it is. The only way to do that is by hard work and perspiration. It's just the way it is, and I'm sure that one of the reasons that I made it in this country was because I sustained my earlier discipline. For me though, it's more than discipline. It's like oxygen and water – I can't do without it. I cannot have a day when I don't do music in one way or another.

By 1963, all these big spectacular shows took a nose-dive because of the recession which hit the country. They tried valiantly at Channel Seven to continue this kind of high-powered, high standard musical show. John Laws compared a terrific show for some time which was called 'Music Time'. It went on for about a year I think, and then it was fazed out because the money wasn't readily available. You can imagine the amount of money that was spent on a thirty-six piece orchestra, thirty piece choir, and choreographers, orchestrators, costume designers, wardrobes, and sets. They obviously rationalised and cut costs. It became much smaller. In fact very, very small until it became 'The Mavis Bramston Show', which had a quintet music group and featured stars like Gordon Chater, June Salter, Carol Ray and Barry Creyton.

This show was video-taped on a Tuesday night, and on Wednesday nights it was replayed nationally. Television was still black and white but, at least by now, it was linked into national networks. 'The Mavis Bramston Show' started out as a trial, in the same format as David Frost's show in England called, 'This Was The Week That Was'. It had some very clever script writers and comedy writers. People wanted to know who Mavis Bramston was, and script writers said, 'We don't know.' It was just a name. They eventually created a character, who was originally played by Noelene Brown and Maggie Dense – I'm not sure who was first. She was presented as a ridiculous theatrical woman, totally untalented. It started out as a pilot show and this is an example of how a fairly experienced man like myself could fall into a heap. When somebody asked me, 'Well, what do you think?' after taping the pilot in front of an audience. I said, 'It will never succeed here.'

It went on for four and a half years and it stopped Australia on Wednesday nights. It was the first time that Australian audiences were able to hear risque humour and words like 'bum,' and all kinds of political and religious satire. It was outrageous in the context of the times, totally open, suggestive and radical, and there was a sketch which was to become notorious called 'The Flower Arrangement'.

On one occasion, Ampol Petroleum had sponsored the show and that particular sketch was shown. The next day, Bishop Muldoon, a Roman Catholic Bishop, said, 'Every God-fearing, good Roman Catholic should never buy Ampol Petroleum again.' If you saw the sketch now you would wonder what was so upsetting about it. It was simply a husband and wife sitting on a couch; she was reading a book called 'Flower Arrangement' and he was reading a book which was obviously a bit racy and would allow for the sexual innuendo which was to follow. The wife said, 'Isn't that interesting? You put this stem into this bit here.' And her husband looked shocked, and exclaimed, 'That's filthy!' Everything she said had a double meaning and he totally misconstrued it. She was

My Parents.

Myself, in an early performance, aged 1 and 1/2.

Aged 2 and 1/2, already precocious.

My sister Marianne and I.

In front of the apartment building where we lived in Budapest. My sweet tooth was evident even then.

By 16,
I was an
accomplished
concert
pianist.

My beautiful sister.

*The very first band. Gabor
Reeves is in front with clarinet,
I am at the piano.*

*The Filu Orchestra, at the Kit
Kat Club, our first
professional engagement.*

The Szepsi Orchestra, Teheran,
1948. Jules Szepsi the band
leader is on the extreme right.

Eve and I in 1956.

Sydney, 1956.

1959, The ATN Channel 7 Orchestra

Stan Freeberg, one of the world's greatest stand up comics, his wife, Eve and myself. This was taken in 1960 during the filming of a TV special.

Recording the first of many film scores at Channel 7.

The very versatile Channel 7 Orchestra. Here we were trying to look like New Orleans jazz musicians.

Rehearsing with Col Joye.

A recording session with Johnny O'Keefe.

Sharing a joke with Bing's brother, Bob Crosby.

*"The Velvet Fog',
Mel Torme.*

*The legendary jazz musician
Dave Bruebeck.*

My friend Winnie Atwell.

The famous radio personality, Jack Davy, with visiting jazz singer Billy Eckstein.

Jack Davy hosted a live radio breakfast show on 2GB which featured many visiting artists, such as Sammy Davis Junior.

George Shearing was one of the finest jazz pianists in the world and working with him was a great honor. Here we are discussing the arrangement he was to perform.

Jack Benny and Jerry Lewis. Two very special people whom I am honoured to call friends.

This is the group of friends, family and colleagues that appeared with me on
'This Is Your Life' program in 1967.
From left to right:
Bob Gunn, my then manager;
Frank Strain, producer of Channel 7's 'Sydney Tonight' program during the
early years;
Claire Poole, my dear friend and colleague, leader of the Claire Poole Singers;
David Sale, head script writer for the Mavis Bramston Show;
Carol Raye, actress and star of the Mavis Bramston Show;
Werner Baer, Music Supervisor of the ABC;
Eric 'Boof' Thomson, for years my principal trumpet player;
Gabor Reeves, my longtime friend;
Digby Wolfe, the presenter;
and my family, Eve, Dory, Vicky, and Dory's daughter Cherie.

Royal Command Performance for Prince Charles at the Sydney Opera House, 1977.

Rehearsing for the Royal Command Variety Show at the Sydney Opera House in 1980.

Presentation to the Queen after the concert.

This was taken during an historic moment in the EMI studios in Sydney where, for the first time, Australia and Britain were linked by the magic of satellite. We were recording a song I composed for the motion picture called 'Barney'. The orchestra and I played the backing in the Sydney studio, it was relayed by satellite to the London Studio where Julie Anthony sang the lyrics. Her voice was then relayed back to us in Sydney and it was recorded simultaneously in both studios.

This was taken in 1980, about 8 weeks after my first heart bypass operation. At the time I was engaged to conduct a special series called 'Cabaret' on the recently formed SBS Channel. When asked if I could conduct so soon after the operation, my surgeon said to me 'Tom, if you couldn't, the operation was a failure'. But as you can see, I was a bit nervous.

In 1982, the Commonwealth Games Year in Brisbane culminated in the Second Royal Command Variety Performance at Her Majesty's Theatre. Hugh Cornish, an accomplished pianist as well as the executive producer of the program and myself presented a performance called 'Duelling Pianos'. It began with just the two of us on stage and then the curtain was raised to reveal another 8 pianos. 4 playing with me and 4 with Hugh. This was my daughter Vicky's first public performance. She is seated above me.

Hugh, presenting me to the Queen after this concert. Rolf Harris is on the far left.

David Gray, Vicky and myself in Hobart where we were performing at the Odeon with the Tasmanian Symphony Orchestra.

Vicky giving me some tips during rehearsal.

Vicky and I on a promotional tour with Mike Walsh.

Vicky and I with Don Lane.

Rehearsing for the opening of the Entertainment Centre in Sydney, 1984. Peter Allen is in the centre, next to him is my manager Ken Laing. On the far right is Graeme Lyall, one of the best saxophone players this country has ever produced.

Julie Anthony and Barry Crocker.

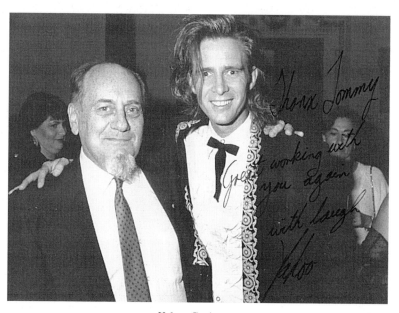

Yahoo Serious.

Daryl Summers and the gang at a concert in Newcastle.

Being presented with the prestigious Mo Award.

It's not Moses parting the Red Sea, but it was still quite a feat conducting such a massive orchestra. This was taken at the benefit concert after the Newcastle earthquake in front of Prince Andrew and an enormous audience.

Rehearsing with the Sydney Symphony Orchestra. Conducting is really only reminding the orchestra of what they have worked through in rehearsals.

I have had such a magnificent life.
Life is good.

innocently reading from a book of flower arrangements. I can't even remember the sketch fully but it was totally outrageous for its time. Television was very heavily censored: you certainly could not say four letter words. Not that I agree with the excessive use of them these days but I think that they can be used if it's important to create a real-life situation. After all, that's the way people sometimes talk when they're angry but if it's just for the sake of saying the words – I find it totally unnecessary and offensive

When I trip over something I say, 'Oh shit!' If that was said on television within the same context nobody would think twice about it, but if you'd said it in those days you would have been arrested. Indeed, at the time when 'Hair' was showing for the first time, people walked away, reeling from seeing a couple of naked bodies on stage. Up to that point, even in the most daring cabaret shows women were permitted to be undressed up top but they had to have a fig leaf or something covering certain parts, and they had to be totally motionless. That was the legislation. They had to stay stock still. If they moved the house manager would be arrested or the place closed down.

That 'Flower Arrangement' sketch catapulted 'The Mavis Bramston Show' into popularity. It became one of the most well-known television shows this country has ever produced. It went on for four and a half years – an incredible success.

It was a huge amount of work for me. Each show had at least seven, and sometimes as many as ten, topical songs or sets of lyrics that various people contributed, and they had to be set to music so that the people could sing them. Not that they were great songs or pop songs or operatic songs; they were set to music so that they were not just poems, which would have been very dry to do. I would get the lyrics for these songs on Tuesday night after we finished the video-taping, which was sometimes as late as midnight. I would go through them with the producer and the head script writer, David Sale. The words were very topical – political things that happened, events in Nicaragua or wherever. He would say, 'This should be like a Samba, because it's South American.'

I wrote all the information down, went home and collapsed into bed. Next morning at about seven-thirty I was up and working again. I started to get the pulse by just reading the lyrics and then the music would come. I don't know how, but it just came, and as soon as it did, I wrote it down and went on to the next song. By seven or eight o'clock at night, sometimes as late as ten o'clock, I had to have all the songs done; because next morning at ten o'clock we started rehearsing with the people in the show. We rehearsed Thursdays, Fridays, and Saturdays. Sunday was a layoff day, and we were back to it on Monday from ten o'clock to six o'clock. On Monday nights I wrote the orchestrations for rehearsal next morning in the studio and we taped in front of a live audience at eight o'clock that night. That's how it went on for four years; it was madness. The preparation was immense because material for the show had to be topical, and sometimes a set of lyrics would be handed to me at eleven o'clock on the morning of video-taping. Sometimes, if a song was really topical, I would get it only an hour before. I would have about half an hour to write the score, another half hour to teach it to the performers and a lunch break to orchestrate it. I was called 'Mr Music'.

The show petered out by itself. It had become repetitive because there was a limit to the number of times they could use the same kind of gag of a political or sexual nature, and eventually it was cancelled. And so we went back to where we had started, with the night shows. Stuart Wagstaff, Tommy Leonetti, Bob Rogers – producers were looking around for anyone who could do it. These were the days before pre-taping. They were actually going to air live and it was a skill, controlling a live show like that; not everyone could do it.

But by then, the night shows themselves were not the same big entertainment that they had been. They went to air at a much later time slot and lacked the big glamour of the early years. I too was becoming jaded and that's when I realised I would have to leave soon and go out into the big brave world of performing in concerts again. I had become so used to this antiseptic world of television, where the audience was not in front of us. We always had a studio audience, maybe 100-200 people, but they were there only as an extra ingredient to provide a planned and prompted response – applause, laughter. It was really a manufactured environment and I knew that sooner or later, I had to get out of it.

One night, I felt I'd had enough of it. By then, the production was reduced to a Tonight Show once a week, and my orchestra had been reduced to a quartet, and I thought, 'I've been here before, about twenty years ago!' And so by mutual agreement between the studio and myself, we parted company.

I had been doing arrangements and recordings outside of Channel Seven for sometime. By then, it was not frowned upon: several years before, they would not have tolerated it and that reminds me of a story. When I first started doing outside work, I took on an alias. I called myself, Henry Connors. Henry, after Henry Mancini, and Connors because that's my wife's family – and I wrote songs and opened a bank account for royalties to go into.

In those days, opening a bank account was as easy as walking into the bank and asking for it. I forgot about the account and it was many years later that Eve reminded me of it. By then, times had changed, and it was a lot harder to get the money out. 'But I am Henry Connors,' I said, and they said, 'No you're not. You're Tommy Tycho.' Eventually they believed me. I had written a song for Jimmy Little – the aboriginal singer – called 'Royal Telephone' which was a world hit, and I had been getting royalties from it and the account was a fairly decent one.

I did this because I was being rebellious: Channel Seven had said that because I was under contract to them, everything I did and wrote was theirs. Of course it wouldn't happen today, but even then, I thought, 'No! How dare they.' The industry was still developing then and the legal issues were just emerging, but there was a tendency to pull your head in and do as you were told. I am not really a rebel – if it's there, it is a subconscious streak. But when I see injustice or stupidity that holds back progress, I get angry, and then I am motivated to do something about it. This decree by Channel Seven seemed to call for some response.

Chapter 8
Life After Television

When I left Channel Seven, early in 1971, I took a year's sabbatical. Leaving the hectic world of television should have been a welcome relief, it should have been great but in fact it was a terrible time for me. I felt empty and spent. I just moped around feeling totally disoriented. I had worked all my adult life at a pace which was insane and to suddenly cut off from the regulated hours and the daily disciplines was, for me, what I imagine it must be like for an addict to suddenly cut off from drugs. I was depressed; I hung around as if my life was in suspended animation, and for a long time I didn't do a damn thing.

In retrospect, I can see that I made some poor judgements because I felt like a fish out of water, and so I leapt at whatever opportunity came my way without giving things proper consideration.

I was asked to be the Musical Director of one of the big RSL clubs. It was not what I would normally have considered but I was persuaded, by the entrepreneur who approached me, that it would be a good thing for me. He said I wouldn't have to do much – just lend my name to the band and occasionally make some appearances playing solos and so on.

On the opening night I did a spot playing solos and attended the reception and everything seemed okay. On the following Saturday as I was about to go out, I received a very tense phone call from the club demanding, 'Where the hell are you? You're meant to be here!' Now this was not my understanding, and when I spoke to the agent who had organised the deal he assured me everything was okay. I went out as planned and had a lovely evening but next morning I got another call from the club saying, 'You're sacked.'

This time, when I rang the agent he just said, 'There seems to be a little misunderstanding. They didn't understand the concept I was selling them.' I realised that he'd lied to both of us – but I learned from that.

Another bad judgement I made concerned an idea that actually sounded okay. The Coogee Bay Hotel wanted a show, and this was being organised by one of the producers of the old Mavis Bramston show. He had the idea of writing a basic boy-meets-girl storyline around a core group of classic old musical songs. It was a reasonable idea but there was not much money in it and we had to use new untested talent. Every night about four people and a dog turned up, and eventually it went bankrupt. That was the other great failure in my life.

It wasn't that I needed to work, but every so often I felt guilty about not working and being so footloose. It was frightening having my life so unplanned. However, as some wise man once said, 'Even the greatest failure can teach you something beneficial.' The benefit for me was in learning to be careful when selecting projects.

It was about this time that I met a man called Mel Welles. He was a genius. He was American, an ex-actor and producer known as 'The Surgeon' in the film world. He was nicknamed The Surgeon because he was called in at the last minute of ailing film productions. He was living in Australia and he came to me, asking to be my manager. His partner, Bob Gunn, was an Englishman. Bob was the administrative man and Mel was the flamboyant, ideas man. The two of them were to be instrumental in getting my career back on track.

As well as becoming my manager, Mel filled in what had been the missing piece in my stage presence. He would say in his American drawl, 'No, Taaahhmy, we have to do it like this,' and I would listen to him because of his experience and his understanding of stagecraft.

I have been fortunate in that I have always had around me the people I needed, when I needed them. Also, I am open to learning from others. I know that I am not an island and there is a lot to learn and so I have always been receptive to new ideas.

Mel and Bob wanted me to do some concerts at the Opera House, which had not long been open. One of the major Sydney radio stations, 2CH, was about to change to an 'easy listening' format, and to capitalise on this they wanted to launch the new format with a series of concerts in the easy listening style. It was Mel who organised it all. The first concert was huge. It was called, '2CH Presents' with Kamahl starring in the program, and it was packed. On the strength of this, these two fellows became my management team and 2CH contracted us to do a series of concerts: 'Tommy Tycho Presents An Evening With Gershwin', or with Cole Porter, with Rogers, Hart, and Hammerstein, with Irving Berlin. They were more that just concerts – they had the radio back-up. Each required months of preparation and then we took the concert touring to each state. They were like a breath of fresh air and it brought me back all to where I had started my career – as a performer in front of a live audience. Like most things, it was not a planned career move; I drifted into it. This was the start of a new phase in my career. But it was not all onwards and upwards: there were a few bad calls in there too.

After the first of these concerts Mel was looking for

something new, and he latched onto an idea which was crazy from the start. The idea was to stage a live 'Horror Show' in a cinema and follow this with a screening of some of the classic old horror movies. He found a cinema owner who was receptive to the idea and concocted this show with lots of dry ice and theatrical tricks. There wasn't much money to spare and so they asked me to compose an accompanying score, which I did. It was recorded, not live, with lots of dramatic organ music. I was there with Eve on the opening night and afterwards I could cheerfully have gone home and smacked my head against a brick wall. It was not just bad, it was truly diabolical – total embarrassment. I felt my reputation was gone, but luckily the show closed after a few days. It was almost as if it vanished without trace, it was so bad.

Some humiliating failures are good experiences. If I had just had successes throughout my whole life I would probably be a most arrogant and childishly confident person. It's good to be brought down to earth a bit.

As a result of all these things, and as a result of the diligence of Mel and his partner – they were both incredibly inventive promoters – a whole range of new opportunities opened up for me. Festival Records made a series of recordings of the Opera House concerts and then they arranged other concerts. One was with Henry Mancini. The first half of the concert featured Barry Crocker, the orchestra, and myself. We were the support act and Mancini was the feature.

And so before too long I was as busy as ever again. It was virtually creating a new market. This idea of symphony orchestras playing light music and aiming to entertain the whole family, instead of just the highbrow few, catered to a totally untapped audience. And it was due to the innovative vision of Mel and Bob.

A huge amount of work went into those concerts; each one was a major production and something of a nightmare to produce. Apart from the technical considerations, I had to rehearse the items with the various solo artists we had chosen. Once this was sitting okay with everyone I would start to write the arrangements. Now, to write an orchestration took the best part of two or three days, and then the orchestral score had to be copied out for the individual musicians and that could mean forty-five to fifty pieces. There were a lot of hours spent in just writing the music, and, when you think that the average song is a few minutes long, and you're doing a two hour concert, it means a lot of work.

I found myself, at times, back to the ten hour and twelve hour days. It was a self-imposed panic this time though, and I learnt just how much I relied on having deadlines to motivate my work. I can recall Eve asking me, 'How do you find the inspiration to write?' and I became aware of how much the deadline helped to manufacture inspiration – the adrenalin starts pumping and sheer necessity is the motivation. It's an excitement in itself knowing that the clock is ticking – it still prevails. I know now that I cannot work when I have a lot of time; I deliberately leave things until I have the pressure of that deadline. I think it's both a natural trait, but also very definitely a result of all those years of producing results on demand for hectic television schedules.

By the mid-70s I was back in full swing, working at a hectic pace. I did concerts in all the major cities. After Gershwin, Cole Porter, Rogers, Hart and Hammerstein and Irving Berlin, we then did a series covering the golden era of the big bands featuring Glen Miller, Tommy Dorsey, Benny Goodman, and Louis Armstrong. That was so successful we did a second series. Then we did another series called, 'By Request' because we couldn't come up with a better title. We toured Australia with each of these concert series. That was between the years 1974-1980. It was Mel who first called me 'Maestro'. I was uncomfortable with it. I squirmed with embarrassment when he first called me that on stage but he said, 'It's show business – every one needs a label,' and so eventually I got used to it and it has become something of a trademark.

My goatee beard is perhaps my best-known trademark. It started out as a practical joke some thirty years ago. In the 1960s there was a show called 'The Mitch Miller Show'. It had a huge cast of singers who, in each performance, sang medleys and solos. One of the soloists was Leslie Uggams and she came to Australia for Channel Seven.

Now, Mitch Miller had a goatee, and as a joke I grew one like it to make her feel at home. I met her at the airport with the official welcoming party and when she saw me she shrieked with laughter. She appreciated it immensely. Then I just became used to it and so it stayed. I would probably have shaved it off after a while – if it hadn't been for my mother. She had been living with us in Australia for some time but had gone back to visit Hungary at the time I grew the goatee.

When she returned, I was there to pick her up. It was a very long trip in those days and her plane had been delayed, and so it was late at night and she was tired. Finally, she got through customs, we collected her luggage and I got her into the car. She relaxed, gave a long sigh and then turned to look at me and screamed. At this point, I had no idea what was wrong. She pointed at me and I looked around wondering what was the matter. Finally, she said, 'What's that? That thing on your chin?'

and I realised what she was pointing at. 'It comes off,' she said. 'No way,' I said. 'It comes off,' she insisted. And I said, 'Mother, I am a grown person. I am the Musical Director of a big company. It does not come off.' She said, 'But it doesn't become you.' And I replied, 'That's beside the point. It stays.' And for many years after, she would shake her head when she looked at me and so it became something of a principle.

Chapter 9
The Music

People often say you need to have a big ego to be in the entertainment business but that's not true. I think I actually have a low self-esteem – being in front of an audience is an acquired skill learned from all these masters; it's not ego. I don't regard what I do as exceptional. I guess it's because it always came so easily and felt so natural. I am doing what I know I do well. When I'm out there, under the spotlight, I deal with it as if I was sitting down talking to someone, one on one.

I don't feel as if I'm better than anyone else. I still feel sometimes – when I'm feeling low as we all do occasionally - that I am deluding myself and deluding all the people who come to hear me. I think, 'Oh God, Maestro! You must be kidding.' There is a story about conductors and their egos, which I recall Andre Kostelanetz recounting in his memoirs. It is about the three most famous conductors in the world, Toscanini, Bernstein, and Von Karajan, and they are engaged in a debate about their expertise in conducting Mozart. 'I've conducted Mozart for many, many years,' said Toscanini, 'and I have no doubt that I am the best qualified to do so.' Bernstein disagreed. 'No,' he countered. 'I was conducting Mozart only last week, and while I was doing so, God himself came to me and said, "Leonard, you are surely the best interpreter of Mozart."' Von Karajan, who had been quiet all this time, studied Bernstein for a moment and then said, 'That's strange. I don't recall speaking to you.'

A really successful concert is reassuring. When a performance goes really well, it's a buzz. I suppose it's connected to wanting to be a perfectionist. There are some performances, perhaps one in every three or four years, when every ingredient comes together and the dynamics work exceptionally well – the orchestra, the soloist, the sound, the lighting, the audience's expectations and response – and it's all working towards the same end. It's magic and you come off the stage afterwards and the feeling...! The elation is incomparable.

This doesn't always happen and there is no formula. It starts when you are waiting in the wings to come on stage. I wouldn't say I get nervous but there is an expectation, an adrenalin surge that's an excitement. It's like walking into a lion's cage and thinking, 'I can conquer this', and I know I can but I'm not 100 per cent sure. However, in the fifty years of my experience there is a trick that I have learned. I stand outside in the wings and the orchestra walks on. They are applauded and they start to tune up. The concert-master walks on and he is applauded, and then, when they are settled, I walk on. This takes several minutes and in this time I am listening to the audience. I can sense their readiness to be entertained or not. If there is animated conversation going on, it comes across backstage as a loud buzz. If there is no buzz I start to think, 'This is going to be hard.'

Strangely enough, there is only one occasion when I can recall a total lack of buzz. It was at the Sydney Opera House. Julie Anthony and I were on the bill and we were standing in the wings and it was deathly silent. Two thousand, six hundred people and no sound. We looked at each other in total panic and she said, 'What are we going to do?' I said, 'We are going to go out there and perform.' We got them in the end but it took so much more energy.

When it's like that you have to be over the top, you have do everything to win them; you sweat like a pig, and that was exactly what I learnt from Jerry Lewis all those years ago.

I am conscious of the response, the first response which tells me that I have been accepted but until then it's like the lion's cage. When I recount this, it sounds like it's terrifying, and in a way I suppose it is, but it is also an excitement which I can only crassly compare to really good sex. You don't know what's going to happen, but when it does happen, it's great. And it has that same kind of satisfaction. When you start with a warm response you ride on that crest and you know that, from there on, you can only go up. And so you are spurred on to do even better, and the energy, the acceptance from the audience is transmitted to the orchestra. And don't forget that the ninety piece orchestra is in itself made up of individuals who may have had a fight with their lover, a toothache, a death in the family or whatever.

The orchestra is an enormously complex animal with its many heads, and to be able to have their undivided attention focused on me takes an enormous amount of energy. Once they have got that buzz from the audience they settle down, and they start to enjoy the fact that they're out there playing. That buzz from the audience is the most important ingredient before I get out on the stage, because if there is no buzz it is terrifying, literally terrifying. I think, 'What the hell am I going to do to get them going?' A lot of times this can happen when there is a sophisticated, bland, blasé audience sitting there who have seen a million concerts and even more musicals. They come in, they've paid their money and they sit down with their arms folded; and their attitude implies, 'Okay, you bastards; entertain me.' You see the boredom on their faces and that's when there is no buzz. That's difficult because you have to win them at all costs, otherwise you've failed.

The best concerts are the ones where the audience is eager, where the tickets have sold out early and so you know there's a keenness. That in itself is a good start, a solid ground to work on. Recently, in New Zealand, I was given a standing ovation when I walked out on stage. Nothing had even happened. That catapults you on to cloud nine; from then on you know that you have them. To use an old show business line: You know that even if you fart on stage, they will applaud! You've won them before you've even started. That has its own set of problems however, because you can easily become over-confident, over-cocky and then you relax too early in the concert, which can lead to disaster. And so, you have to tell yourself, it's still business as usual. You relax slowly until you find that level at which everything is running smoothly.

It is a frightening experience at the best of times; but at the same time it's so exhilarating that I can't describe it adequately, and I know I can't live without it.

Conducting takes a lot of physical energy and a huge amount of mental energy. You have to be two hundred per cent aware of the mental demands, because when you face an audience you loose fifty per cent of your confidence to start with. You have to over-compensate to begin with. I am sure I loose about a kilo and a half every time I conduct a concert. I have been complimented in reviews saying that I have a very easy, laid back and relaxed style of conducting: I learned it from previous experiences.

You don't have to conduct an orchestra all the time. A lot of conductors have a macho, self-important idea that they have to conduct the orchestra all the time, but a lot of the time they get in the way. The orchestra has the music in front of them and they know what they are doing: they wouldn't be sitting there if they weren't qualified to be there. Over-conducting shows a certain distrust on the part of the conductor in not letting the orchestra get on with their job. Conducting is really only guiding. It's not controlling. If you control them, you don't make music.

In fact, conducting in a concert is really only reminding the orchestra of what they have worked through at rehearsals. That's where it all happens. You are reminding them, during the concert, of the sticky phrases that have been difficult and have been overcome in those rehearsals. The reminder is simply a matter of noting, 'Here we go, here comes that difficult part, now watch me'.

The orchestra is just as important, if not more important and integral to the performance, than me waving my arms about. At times, I do that as a joke for the audience when they applaud me, but it's not me, it's the orchestra that does all the work. I just wave my arms around in a silly fashion — the audience laugh at it but that's really what it is. If I don't respect the orchestra, then I don't have their co-operation or their enthusiasm.

Conducting is body language too: you don't have to make big gestures with your arms – it can be with your little finger and they will still respond the same way. Once the pulse has been established, the smallest hand movement is enough to guide them through the next minute, or even two minutes, until the next change of tempo or mood, or change of dynamics or drama comes along – in which case you have to start conducting again. I don't know what it is ultimately that draws all the parts together into a unified whole. It's an instinct and it's something I have been working on for all of my career. If I had the answer, I would write it down and I would probably make a fortune because I know that a lot of other people would also like that question answered.

When you think about it, it is a frightening aggregate of individuals. How they work as one is a mystery. Top class orchestras made up of professional musicians have lots of blood, sweat and tears, and more than a few rehearsals behind them. Not one of the musicians would be there if they hadn't been through that, and so that amount of expertise is very easy to 'guide' They know what is expected of them. It's only a matter of walking up to the podium and saying, 'Okay, we're going to do such and such,' and waiting for them to settle down. You have to give the right hand movement to start the piece, and guide them through the first rehearsal. It will no doubt have certain problems within it and so you stop at the end of the piece and say, 'Right, now, I think we have a bit of a problem in such-and-such a bar. Let's talk about it and work it out.' It's a mater of co-ordinating their problems with my problems and I have never, ever, in my career, simply said, 'Okay brass, you're too bloody loud.' I don't believe you say that to artists – though many conductors do. The problem is that you alienate them then and there.

You can say it in a joking way. 'Hey, brass bullies! Back off, it's too loud!' but that is only when you know them well and have worked together long enough and they know that your manner is not for real. In the beginning you say, 'Excuse me, but I think you are overpowering the strings here. Could you just try maybe forty per cent less in that section?' It's mostly a matter of intelligent banter between them and me. They may ask me certain questions and if I can't answer them, I'm down the tube; they do not respect me. Respect is crucial to any relationship.

You're not always home-free however, even when you have that. If you have a reputation as a good conductor, that can be daunting for a new orchestra. They look at you almost with fear. And so you have to loosen them up. I say, 'Look you guys, I'm here to play music; let's see what you can do.' The first rehearsal is tight – they're expecting criticism and I don't know how good they are. Every first rehearsal is a test case. They're also testing me. They test any conductor; they systematically plan who will make mistakes. It's quite deliberate, and if I don't pick them up, I'm finished. I have to prove how good I am. The fifth cellist will ask, 'Do I have an f sharp here or an f flat?' And I will look at the score and say, 'You have an f sharp but you played an f natural, didn't you?' Then you rehearse the same piece again and from then on, you can see the tension dissolve as they accept you. Initially, it's about relationships but once that rapport is established, it's a real joy because you can get down to the business of creating really good music together.

I am reminded of an anecdote that is attributed to Sir Thomas Beecham. It's said that there was a scheduled rehearsal one particularly foggy London morning and many of the musicians were running late. However, Beecham was a stickler for punctuality and he started the rehearsal on time regardless, and so there were people scurrying in during the first movement, while he was conducting. About three or four minutes into the movement, as the orchestra was swelling in numbers, he yelled out, 'Second trombone, you're too loud.' He kept on conducting and the orchestra kept on playing and the orchestra manager quietly came up behind him and said, 'Sir Thomas, the second trombone player isn't here yet.'. Sir Thomas answered, 'It doesn't matter. When he gets here, tell him he's too loud!'

I make a habit of learning people's names before I get to the first rehearsal. I also make a point of talking to them, getting know them as individuals. I ask for a list of their names and the instruments they play, and, if possible, a photo with each person identified on the back of it. I keep a list of names on the stand at rehearsal and try to use them. I don't have to call out, 'Excuse me, second French horn.' I say, 'Charlie?' and he looks up startled, and I say, 'Charlie, what have you got in bar fifty-nine?' and he tells me. I challenge him. 'Well, you should have such-and-such; is that wrongly played or wrongly copied?' Now I know it's not wrongly copied, but he has an out, and the rest of the orchestra all know that I am aware that he knows. This is what they're listening for – an effort on my behalf to acknowledge them as individuals.

Humour is important in winning an orchestra over, and I keep using my most inane jokes to get them smiling. I check their reaction and if they don't smile I have to keep cajoling until they do. In doing so, we become this magical animal that is the sum of us all and this magic transmits to the audience. I interact with the orchestra a lot during a performance but you see lots of great conductors who do not have this rapport with their orchestras and it's a forbidding sight. The orchestra will bust their gut to play well but there's no rapport. I coax and cajole. I use eye contact and body language. When we come up to a difficult piece that the brass has had problems with, and they get it right, I give them the thumbs up, I acknowledge that they've done well. When I look at the cello section which is to my right, I turn to them and I smile. It cannot be done, of course, in a dramatic work like Bruckner, or Mahler or Beethoven where the drama is so heavy, like molasses. You can't do that, it would be crass and vulgar. But in light music where there are lots of smiles anyway, it's perfect.

In my reviews it's often said that we look like we are having fun and we are enjoying ourselves. The audience shares that too. Solo artists have to be drawn into the whole and so I also try to involve them. I smile at them and nod at them. I acknowledge them.

Every concert has its own highs and lows. There is always the threat of disaster, especially as equipment becomes more complex and technical. Sometimes, however, you can't blame technical problems; it's the human element. I remember one concert which was in the Melbourne Town Hall and was being broadcast throughout Victoria. The MC and I agreed that he would call me to the microphone and I would announce some of the soloists. I began this by telling the audience that I appreciated the chance to talk to them instead of just having my back to them for the whole concert, and that it was important to me to dispel the rumour that musicians were "dumb". I then proceeded to introduce one of the soloists, Penny Hay, and I walked back to the podium where I discovered from my notes that I had just introduced the wrong person. There was nothing else to do except walk back to the microphone and admit, 'Who says I'm not dumb?' The audience laughed, I got the intro right for Don Cant and it all went well, but for a moment there I know I caused absolute panic backstage.

Thinking on your feet is one thing you have to learn it's the ability to cover your mistakes. Having done so many concerts and live performances, and television performances and interviews, it's something I can do. It's mostly self-depreciating humour, and that's okay because audiences like to see that you're human. After the antiseptic world of television, the world of live performances was scary. It was absolute panic for me, but now, I am very comfortable with it.

I am reminded of an incident which happened many years ago when I was taking 'The Tommy Tycho Night with George Gershwin Show' to Adelaide. We had the same cast travel with us to all the locations, except for the compere, who was Len London, a Sydney radio personality in those days. I never spoke on stage back then, I always used a compere. We had the script, and everyone else was very familiar with the program, and so we just slotted in a new compere for this show.

Everything ran very smoothly but for one oversight. No one had told our new compere that at the end of the show, just before we did 'Rhapsody in Blue', I would go offstage while he was talking and change from my usual black dinner suit, black shoes and black tie, into an all white outfit. The time came, and I walked offstage to where my dresser was waiting in the wings, and the compere began to talk about 'Rhapsody in Blue' and how this was the last piece. It was all according to the script but he was going at 500 miles an hour!

The moment he started, I realised that I had not warned him to slow this down to give me the minute and a half that I needed to get changed. We had this timed to perfection but he was announcing me and I was still only half dressed. In show business, when they announce you, you have to get out there on the stage quickly, or else it looks like something is wrong. My dresser was panicking, I was panicking. I had my shoes and socks on, I had just put the tie on and was pulling my trousers up while the dresser was pushing my arms into the coat. I went out there, not realising that my fly was undone all the way. As I was taking my bow, I looked down and, to my horror, saw that it was open.

Fortunately, with a white shirt against the white trousers, it was not obvious to the world. I turned and walked back from the front of the stage to the piano; I was desperately trying to pull up the zipper and it got stuck on the shirt. It was like a nightmare. There was nothing I could do and so I sat down at the piano and started playing. Each time there was the orchestral section and I wasn't playing, I turned away from the audience and with one hand I was conducting the orchestra and with the other I was trying to free the zipper.

A couple of orchestra members could see what was going on and they nudged or nodded to their fellows and so gradually, the whole orchestra became aware of my predicament. The 'Rhapsody' goes for about fourteen minutes, and each time I turned to face them I continued the desperate, one-handed battle with my zipper. I was conscious of their mirth and that made matters worse. I couldn't budge it.

We finished the piece and I stood up and took my bow with my two hands clasped in front of me. I walked off stage, with the audience none the wiser, and pulled the bloody thing up! I could almost hear the roars of laughter from the orchestra. It was hilarious, in hindsight, but at the time it was terrible. Musicians have a twisted sense of humour.

These types of things can only happen when you work live and that's why I love it so much. But a concert, a recording, a film score – I can't make the distinction between them in terms of preference; they each have their own attraction and built-in enchantment.

The recording process is one that I enjoy because if you do a good recording, it will be there forever. You can't erase mistakes from a recording. The only way is to do take after take until you do it so well it's a perfect take. In music circles I am proud to be known as 'One Take Tycho'. Most of my recordings I can do in one take, because I know through experience how far I have to go, how much energy I need, to attain that high pitch of excitement, of involvement, from the orchestra and the singers. It may take twenty minutes, it may take an hour, but there's a moment when it just comes together and then I can say, 'Okay, now, let's record it.'

When that occasional thing goes wrong and we have to do another take, I look around at the orchestra and I say, 'You just ruined my reputation.' If you capture a good performance there is an immense feeling of satisfaction, but if it's less than perfect, if you let a mistake remain on a record, it's a blemish that's there forever. The first time you hear it it's irritating, the second time you hear it it's even more irritating, and the fiftieth time you hear it you want to smash the record it's so bad. It gets magnified with each playing.

I try to learn from my recordings. I ask for copies of broadcasting tapes and listen to all of them by myself at home, critically, and see what I have done and what I could improve. I make mental notes all the time. 'The next time I do this piece, I must do it differently,' I say to myself. 'It does not work how I imagined it to. It sounds dragging, or it sounds pompous.' I constantly try to improve.

It is hard to say what my favourite recordings are, but if I think about it, it would have to be the last ones that I did with Anthony Warlow. First of all, because there was virtually an unlimited budget the pressure was off. There was no sense of: 'We've got to finish this tonight or else'. Then there was the fact that his artistry is immense: his experience, his sense of timing, his sense of style, his musicality is unparalleled in this country. He was a joy to work with.

As well as this, I had the Melbourne Symphony Orchestra with not only their professional pride, but every ounce of their talent, backing Anthony's comeback in a personal way. Additionally, we had the best studio in the country and the best sound engineer, Robin Gray at the Allan Eaton studios in Melbourne. All the ingredients were there; it was like going to heaven. There was one session when we did only one track in three hours – which is an unheard-of luxury. I was almost apologising for the time it was taking but it wasn't a problem. We worked together for months to perfect it, and the end result was that his voice was enveloped and enhanced by the backing. It was a joy. A simple joy.

Film scores are a different matter for me. I have been frustrated by the fact that even though I put all of my ability into writing the scores, the films themselves have not become the huge successes I had hoped. Writing a film score is a co-operative thing between the producer, the director, and myself to work out where the music should be. That's not automatically agreed and so there is a fair amount of discussion at that stage. Sometimes it comes down to a practical rationalisation: the director may say, for example, 'We need strong music in this scene because the acting is a bit weaker.'

By this stage, the film is almost completely shot and substantially edited. This is another frustration in writing a film score – with very few exceptions, the music composer is presented with a final product. There is no leeway for you to put your own musical stamp on it. You are hampered by the length of scenes. And so that even if you feel there is a nice musical phrase you would like to finish, you have to chop it before its logical end because of the length of the scene. It's an incredibly frustrating chore, fitting the music to pre-set times. For instance, if there is a hero, and every time he appears you want to herald him by playing a phrase that is a theme for this character, this might work most of the time, but then there is one scene where you can't do it because the scene is too short. It's a very mechanical process, you virtually go through the film, scene by scene, and calculate, for example, that in this section the music needs to run for seventeen and a half seconds and it's dramatic, while another this section requires the love theme and it has a different length of time.

Then you need to remember too, that the music is almost always subliminal, unless the director dictates otherwise, and then you have the music soaring over the scene in a way that dominates it. You go fully symphonic and write your best, most passionate melodies. However, mostly you have to subjugate your craft to the point where you are really using musical noises to underscore a scene. You're subservient to the image and the sound effects and the dialogue. It's very difficult. Think of any action scene: there is usually some very exciting music, but mostly it's swamped by the sounds of tyres screeching, or whatever action is happening and so you don't actually listen to the music. But if it wasn't there, the impact of the scene would be lost.

It is difficult too because you are writing to the dictates of the producer and director. Sometimes you do some great work and they say, 'No, that's not what we want. We want something like this,' and so you go home and rewrite it. I have yet to come across a producer who is musically articulate. They know it when they hear it, but they can't describe it beforehand.

Spielberg is the exception. I think he is very musically

articulate, and I believe he also works with the score before the film is shot. This allows for flexibility. If the composer wants to finish a phrase, the scene can accommodate an extra three or five seconds. Because of this, you see films like 'Jaws', 'E.T.', 'Schindler's List', and you cry. The music is subliminal, it enhances and supports the emotion and the drama on the screen. It doesn't dominate the images but it lifts you right out of your seat. In these films, the artistic integrity of the whole film is intact and that's what the audience responds to. In themselves, the best scores have an internal logical development, not a piecemeal fragmentation.

When I was very young, I was interested in stage design, and art, and drawing, but I think that was just a curiosity about the other arts. As much as I love films, I don't think I would want to, or be able to, direct one myself. I can respect the huge amount of experience and the craftsmanship involved in such a task. Now writing music, for instance, is something that I know I have a certain amount of expertise in, although I don't believe I am necessarily good at it. One of the reasons I have not composed much music for posterity is that I don't believe in adding to the existing music library of the world just for the sake of saying, 'Look, I have written a symphony, aren't I good?'

It's not so much that I have nothing to say, more that because of the way I have worked, I have never had the luxury of unlimited time to sit and compose something so good I could be happy with it. All of the work I have done has been commissioned for specific people or events, and I would love to have the luxury of just writing for the sake of it, but I don't know if I would be good enough or if I could do it without my usual work pattern with its deadline pressure.

For myself, I don't believe it's important to leave something for posterity: once I'm gone, I'm gone. If I had an overwhelming urge to write, I would, but the pieces I have done do not inspire me. One composition I did was for the West Australian Symphony Orchestra, a piece called 'A Prom Overture'. It's a nice piece but when I hear it I think, 'Alright, I can hear a bit of Wagner here and a bit of Mozart there and a bit of this and that,' and it's very pleasant but if it is never heard again, no problem.

What I seem to be doing is satisfying my whole artistic range, not focusing on one area. I think there is a lot of music that is garbage and would be better of it wasn't written. I don't believe there is much good new music around. At the moment, music and culture are in the doldrums. I am talking in general: we are going through a terrible phase where people don't know where they are going. Things are changing at an alarming speed. I mean electronics, science, life in general. All these things have invaded our homes and we don't know how to deal with them.

Artistically, today there is no way of extending oneself. Two hundred years ago Beethoven, Mozart, Haydn, Handel and Brahms had the times of their lives spending hours, weeks, even months, finishing off one movement. They could do this because there was no hurry. Beethoven rewrote 'The Fifth Symphony' four times: that would have taken about three years. The pace of life today does not allow you that amount of time to sit and deliberate – unless you write for art's sake, not caring if it's a piece that ever finds an audience. If I have a film score that needs to be finished I sometimes only have three days to do it in. This pressure of time means we compromise; there is no time to perfect things. There is nothing productive happening in the arts. What there is, is very experimental and it's so hard to play. I pity the poor musicians who have to play it. I once heard this story. Sir Thomas Beecham was asked by a reporter whether he had conducted Stockhausen (the current contemporary classical composer). Sir Thomas, with his extraordinary wit replied, 'No, but I've trod in a lot of it!'.

Even worse than contemporary classical music is today's rock music. I find it degrading. It has insufficient to say and it is just a very basic, banal noise. That's without even mentioning the ludicrous lyrics. They don't show any musical integrity. Take something like rap music – I don't know how they even dare to call it music, it is nothing like music at all. I am now old enough and bold enough to say these things. There was a time when I would have kept my opinions to myself, but now I say what I think and if it offends people well, I'm sorry for that, but this is truly what I think. I see so much on television, and hear so much on radio these days that is nothing but crap. Michael Jackson, for instance – he may well be a good dancer but he cannot sing to save himself, and the performances he offers are not artistic, they're bullshit. It's not music, it's not art, it's nothing!

It irritates me that such people are put on a pedestal. It is not honest and it has more to do with big business that art. A big record company goes out into the street and picks out four boys and says, 'Here is our new rock group'. I even dispute the integrity of a band like the Beatles. I cannot believe that those four boys wrote all the compositions that they claim to have written. When you look at the musical style, there are two or three songs that they could never have written. Songs like 'Yesterday', 'Michelle', and 'Norwegian Wood' are sophisticated, good pieces of music and I doubt they were written by someone who did not have a sound, professionally trained musical background. Not in a hundred years!

I think there is something basically wrong with the world that the marketing machines can do this. It bothers me because I think that about ninety-six per cent of the world is musically illiterate, and it is this market that is being exploited. It is almost as if they say, 'Here, this rubbish is good enough for you, you stupid idiots'. It used to worry me a lot; now I think it irritates me more than anything because I know I can't change it. No one can change it: it's being driven by the God Almighty dollar. I think it's a terrible indictment of the world today. I sometimes look at young people, say a pianist on the 'Quest' program, who has huge talent – far more than a handful of these superstars put together – and I know that if he sticks with it, he will be battling for twenty years to make a go of it. Where is the justice in that?

Education is vital. The biggest problem is that people are just not exposed to real music. I don't think they have to be taught it, they just need to hear it because something good is good, regardless of changing music styles. Movies like 'Amadeus' are wonderful because that one movie alone had thousands of young people sitting and listening to Mozart. When Eve and I went to see that movie we sat in the same row as some young people with green and orange spiky hair and they sat there, open-mouthed. These were people you would never expect to find in a symphony concert, but here they were enjoying classical music.

In recent years there has been something of a revival of Glen Miller music, and people who have never heard it before, discover it and say, 'Wow! This is good stuff!' I abhor the elitist approach and attitude of those people who want to keep music away from the people. Light music is a good bridge that can lead people to learn more about classical music.

Light music is more accessible to audiences who are not musically educated. From television, movies, department store muzak, etc., people are exposed to lots of music. A light music concert builds on what they are already familiar with, and I would hope, adds to their education. The appreciation from people who come to my concerts and have not been exposed to live orchestral music before is overwhelming. They hear the great tidal wave of sound of the orchestra and it is a new experience for them.

The Melbourne Symphony Orchestra also deserves full credit because they have been doing so many things that orchestras traditionally wouldn't do. They have done tours with artists like Elton John, John Farnham, and Frank Sinatra, and lots of film scores. They are enjoying it and getting a wider audience too. They are wonderful!

I am not intelligent enough or clever enough to try to predict the future of the arts, or even music in this country. People keep pointing to new developments and saying, 'This is the new thing' but invariably it's not.

Chapter 10
The People

Julie Anthony, Anthony Warlow, Jackie Love, Yahoo Serious, Peter Allen, Perry Como.

Julie Anthony is one of the people I am said to have discovered. I hate the expression "discovered" because one doesn't "discover" people. I don't claim that. It's more accurate to say that I was instrumental in nurturing a talent. "Discovering" means a Svengali sort of relationship. I am not being falsely humble. Julie was introduced to me by Tony Brady, who is still her agent and the talent co-ordinator of the Kevin Jacobsen Organisation, one of the big promoters in this country.

When I met her, she was a nineteen year old lass from Gulga in South Australia and she had come to the big smoke after winning a couple of talent shows in Adelaide. She had appeared on a few things like 'The Ernie Sigley Show'. Tony had met her in Adelaide and brought her to Sydney. He rang me one day and said I simply had to hear her. I always tried to help where I could, to give young people a hand to get started and so I agreed and a date was set for them to meet me at my home.

At the time, I had a beautiful Alsatian dog called Fritz who, unfortunately, was prone to killing other animals. He wasn't a vicious dog, in fact he was an absolute sook, but he was very jealous and would attack other cats and dogs at the drop of a hat. We had a large, fenced backyard and he wasn't allowed out of it. He was also clever, and on this particular day, he had managed to open the back door and, unbeknown to me, was lurking in the kitchen.

The doorbell rang, and I opened the door to this young lady who said, 'Hello. My name is Julie Anthony,' and at that point, Fritz, like a tornado flew past us, out into the street. 'Excuse me,' I said, and dived after him. Too late: a little old lady was walking past with her little dog. Fritz seized the dog, the lady was screaming, Fritz was growling and the little dog was making awful noises. I grabbed hold of Fritz's hind legs to make him let go. I was holding on for dear life. I dragged him by his collar back to the house.

We just made it to the top of the steps and, by this time, the little dog had recovered. He was not exactly little, but he was smaller than Fritz, who was huge, and he pulled away from the little old lady, who fell flat on her face and he came flying up the steps determined to finish things with Fritz. So there I was, trying to drag Fritz inside and fend off this other dog who was snapping at Fritz but mostly biting me. Finally he beat a retreat and I got Fritz safely into the backyard. When I looked down, I saw that I was covered in blood from the cuts on my wrists and ankles. I walked back inside and there was Julie, wide eyed and pale. She said, 'What can I do?' She found bandages and wrapped my cuts, and at that moment Tony arrived and asked what happened. He drove me to the hospital where they gave me a tetanus shot and a few stitches.

After all that excitement we ended up sitting at the piano – me in shorts and singlet with all the bandages on, and I said, 'Sing something.' Despite the fact that she was still shaken from recent events, she did, and I tell you she knocked me flat. She was absolutely sensational. I agreed to arrange a couple of songs for her to sing on Channel

Seven, and the first time she was on, the phones rang hot: she was a huge success. I am still very close to her. I am godfather to her first daughter and we are very good friends. We always have been, from that first moment on, and we always will be.

Just as a note to that story: I had to play a piano solo that same evening on the show, and I could not hide all my bandages. Bob Rogers was the compere then, I think, and as he did my introduction he delightedly recounted the whole story for the benefit of the audience. It was one of those moments that you never live down.

Anthony Warlow was already a big name when we met, and we became friends. I created two records for him, and one has gone platinum, and one gold. We worked very closely together creating performances: we selected music together, and I arranged and conducted. As you know, Anthony had a time when he was very ill. We had worked together on several things prior to that. And when he came out of treatment, it just so happened that I was working on the score for the film 'Reckless Kelly' and Yahoo Serious said to me, 'I want Anthony Warlow to sing a song.' I rang Anthony to see if he was able to and he said he would love to. Yahoo wrote the lyrics, which he changed about 500 times and I wrote the music which I changed about 500 times and we came up with a song that Anthony loved.

After that Anthony came back with his manager and we talked about the record he wanted to do. After a long long process we came up with a plan that suited his record company, his manager, himself and me. It was complicated, and the title was to be 'Back In The Swing,' a reference both to his being back from his illness, and also to the type of music he wanted to sing. We then spent a lot of time selecting the songs and orchestrating and rehearsing, and it was recorded in Melbourne with the Melbourne Symphony Orchestra and a big jazz band of over 110 musicians. His management had organised a big promotion on television, and to show the people in Australia that he was fine and well and singing again they said 'Okay, now let's do a big tour around Australia.' And that's what happened. We did twenty-one concerts in twenty-four days, and four days later I had a heart attack, but that's another story.

I loved working with Anthony, and we are still friends. We have gone separate ways but I think our paths will cross every so often.

With Jackie Love, it was different. She was only about sixteen when I met her. She was seen by my manager at the time, Lin Rich. Lin had become my manager after Mel went back to America. He was originally my drummer and he was a real rough diamond. Unfortunately, he was killed in a car accident about fifteen years ago, and then Ken Laing, who was already working for him, took over. So it was Lin Rich who first heard Jackie sing, in Perth and he came back raving about her. We asked her to come over to Sydney, and she and her mother came, they drove across the Nullarbor – what a trip! But when I heard her I thought, 'Wow, she's good.'

At that time, I was the Musical Director for a show called 'Cabaret' which was on Channel O, the predecessor to SBS. It was a musical program that allowed the talent from ethnic groups to be showcased. Turks, and Greeks and people from all over the world. My good friend Claire Poole, who led the Claire Poole Singers on that show, took Jackie on as a backup singer.

One day the producer of the show pulled me aside and said, pointing to her, 'That girl, the one with legs up to her armpits, can she do a solo?' I said ' Of course,' and the next week when she did her song, the phones rang hot. She was a sensation. Soon after that we heard that Sammy Davis Jnr was to come to Australia in about six months time, and he was looking for a support singer. My young manager Lin sent them a tape of Jackie and the answer came back almost immediately: 'We want her.'

And so, for the next six months, we worked hard. I taught her what I knew about how to behave on stage – what to say, what to sing. The opening night came, and after the third song, the blasé, been-everywhere, heard-everything, seen-everything media gave her a standing ovation. After the third song! She continued her performance and she was just a sensation. The crowd was hysterical. When Sammy finally came on his first words were 'How do you follow that?' I was sitting in the crowd, at first worried sick, and then as proud as a parent.

There were others – Diana Trask was one. She came up from Melbourne and worked with me on various things. This was the time when Frank Sinatra came out from America and was performing at the Stadium. (It was pulled down many years ago, but for a long time the Stadium at Rushcutters Bay in Sydney was the biggest entertainment venue available. It usually housed a boxing ring which was converted into a stage for the big performers.) Lee Gordon, the promoter, rang me on this occasion and said he needed a good looking girl to open the show. I recommended Diana, and she was fantastic. Sinatra walked in after the show and said, 'Hey kid, you were great. Come with me to America.' And she did. She became a Country and Western singer.

And so, 'discover'? Maybe: but it's more like fostering a talent. I get them concerts, performances, exposure; I arrange music and I can pass on the stagecraft I have learnt. I think it is important to pass on my experience. I have worked like this with many; at the moment there is a talented young lady from Adelaide called Penny Hay, who has done many performances with me recently. But many people don't make it and, yes, it is disappointing when they don't. It's not because I have failed, or because they have failed, they still have the talent.

There was one girl who showed all the talent in the world, but she was headstrong and she wanted to impose her own tastes on the world. I would say to her, 'You cannot educate an audience: you have to entertain them.' But she would say, 'No, I want them to hear these songs because I like them.' And I would say, 'Whether you like them or not is of no consequence: they've got to like them.' It is disappointing to see the potential and to not see the follow-through.

This is different from managing careers. I don't know how to manage: that's a different kind of marketing strategy. What I can teach these people is a way to sing a song; I stop them and say, 'No, no, no. You have to sing this like so.' I can't sing but I can tell them how to sing. I can suggest that we take it up a key, and make it more dynamic or slow it down a bit. In other words, I am shaping and forming the song in a way that would be advantageous for that singer but I'm not teaching them how to sing. I am just creating a successful performance. It's more than music, it's entertainment.

With Anthony Warlow, for instance, when we came to doing the concerts, he was uncomfortable. Because up until then his stage work had been largely in character – 'Guys and Dolls', 'Les Miserables', 'The Phantom'. In all of these he had a different persona when he walked out on stage; it wasn't Anthony Warlow. Now, all of a sudden, this was Anthony Warlow in concert – "naked" as it were. And so we spent a lot of time talking about ideas. He would say, 'What if I say this?' and I would make suggestions and add comments. One thing we talked about was the idea of including a section where he would talk about his life – how he started singing etc. – and do bits and pieces of songs that were significant in his life. This was to be a very informal section, where he would sit and talk to the audience under a single spotlight.

He had related to me an incident from his audition for 'The Phantom' and we discussed how he should do it in the show. Anthony is a great mimic. He has that ability to listen to a person for just a few minutes and then mimic them perfectly. And so I asked him if he could mimic Michael Crawford's famous television character: the intense, infuriatingly incompetent 'Frank' from 'Some Mothers Do Have 'Em'. Of course, he could do the impersonation perfectly, but it took me ages to persuade him he should do it for the audience. Finally, he agreed, and so in the show he told the story of how he was waiting in the wings for his turn to do this audition. He made a joke about how he had already burnt half of his face with a blow torch for authenticity before it was his turn to walk on. He talked about how the director and producer were somewhere out there in the darkness, and then he proceeded to recount his whole audition in that funny 'Frank' voice. The audience shrieked and so he kept on doing it.

Some of the best gags are the oldest gags in the world. For example, in the introduction to one song Anthony was sitting at the piano, picked up some music, looked at it and said, 'We're not singing Paganini?' and I just motioned to him to turn the page up the other way and he said, 'Oh, page nine; upside down it looked like Paganini! I'm sorry!' It's an old one but it still brings the house down. After the first concert, he felt at home but until then, it was unfamiliar ground for him. While for me, it was what I had learnt way back – as old as vaudeville. He had naturally good timing. It was from being an actor, I suppose.

He had discovered a cassette of himself singing at about age four and I suggested that he use it in the show: he could talk about how he had always wanted to sing from such an early age, and then he could have this tape with his voice come over the loud speakers. He could listen critically to himself singing and say, 'Come on boy, you can sing better, and then he could pick up the song where the boy left off and the orchestra could come in and finish it with a completeness. It was a little show business "shtick" but it worked beautifully.

I suppose this is, after all, what I have to give. It's my trade and it's fifty years experience that I learned from artists like Shirley Bassey and Louis Armstrong. I have learned when I worked with these people I didn't just sit there playing music: I was watching them, what they did, how they did it – and remembering things such as Jack Benny's timing. It is so much more than music, it's entertainment.

Just recently, I was compering my own concerts in Auckland, where I was performing with the Symphony Orchestra, and I realised how natural it all has become for me. I do not need to work with a script, I just talk to the audience and I make jokes and although I am no comic, I make them laugh. It certainly wasn't always like that for me.

Musicians generally are "dumb" on stage. They tend to talk with their music, but few of them are eloquent speakers as well. There are, of course, exceptions – James Morrison and Don Burrows are two that spring to mind – but, in general, they aren't. I never spoke much on stage either (I did in interviews but that was different).

Until one New Year's Eve when, three days before a concert at the Town Hall, the MC had an accident and couldn't show. Because of the time of year, everyone whom I could think of was booked, busy or away, and so they said, 'Tommy, you do it.' My first response was 'Hell no!' but then I thought about it, and thought, 'Well, why not?' And so I reconsidered and said I'd do it. But the moment I said that, I almost I shat myself and thought, 'Oh no, why on earth did I do that?' It came to the last day and we were dressing for rehearsal and one of the musicians asked, 'Who is going to be the MC?' and when I said it was me all the musicians roared with laughter and said, 'You! You must be joking!'

I knew what the items were, I didn't prepare anything I was going to say, and it was a huge success. And now I have become comfortable with it. In New Zealand I recently did a concert with two singers which was called 'Broadway Broads' because it had all the great hits from that era, and when I was introducing the singers I would comment on the title and say that if I had my way I would have called it, 'Broadway Ladies'. I said this with mock seriousness, but throughout the show, every time I referred to them, I deliberately tripped over my own tongue, calling them 'The Broadway Br.., I mean, Ladies.' It was something of a running joke. It got funnier every time I did it as the audience caught on.

In the same show I adapted an old joke which I recall Jerry Lewis using twenty years ago, about America's major cultural contributions to the world being the Broadway Musical, the Motion Picture Industry and Macdonald's. In his day it was Coca Cola. It still works and it's still perfectly applicable.

Over the years, I have worked with some amazing people. One of the most interesting people would have to be Yahoo Serious: he's a crazy man, I have a great deal of affection for him.

I met him when Eve and I had sold our house in Seaforth where we had lived for more than thirty years. We had thirty years of hoarding to sort through, and just as we were about to start packing, this young man knocked on the door and introduced himself as Yahoo Serious and said, 'You must write the music for my film.' I said, 'Pardon?' We discussed it, and I thanked him but explained that I was moving and didn't have the time right then, but he was adamant he wanted me to do it. He had fourteen days in which to get it written and recorded so that he could take the film with him to Los Angeles.

Finally he wore me down and I agreed. And so we moved and the first things that were moved were the piano and the video recorder and I did absolutely nothing except sit in that room from seven in the morning until midnight for the following week. Then I flew to Melbourne to record it, and then the sound was mixed. The deadline was looming. Yahoo's Los Angeles flight left at seven o'clock that night, and the last mix was completed at 5.00 p.m. We just made it.

It's a major achievement: at over fifty minutes of music, it is the equivalent of one and a half Symphonies. When I finished it I thought, 'Never again!' but, in fact, I did it again for Yahoo's next movie, 'Reckless Kelly.' And that time there was an even shorter the lead time. (This is what I mean about the film score being the element that is tacked on at the end. There is never enough time to do it justice.) But I am very fond of Yahoo. I love him. He's a wild and crazy man, a self made man, and I would love to work with him again. He is totally, utterly dedicated: he lives and breathes his work and is always open to learning. He has learnt a lot about music doing these two films.

Peter Allen was another performer with whom I had a long association. When I first met Peter he was performing in a duo called 'The Allen brother'. They were two boys who were friends, but they weren't brothers. One played the guitar and one played the piano. They were called 'The Allen Brothers' because even at the age of 12 or 13, Peter was a showman, and he was the driving force of the pair.

There was a show on Channel Seven at that time called 'Teen Time', which was on once a week and featured a lot of up and coming young performers. I was the musical director for the show and so I worked with the two boys and did some arrangements for them. Peter was very talented then; you could see then that he had something extra about him. It was on Bandstand, on Channel Nine that they really made their mark, and at age 17 or 18 they decided to go and see the world. Their break came when they were introduced to Judy Garland through whom Peter eventually met and married Lisa Minelli.

He was far more talented than many people give him credit for. He was a great song writer. He wrote many songs for many people, including the big hit, 'I Love You, I Honestly Love You' for Olivia Newton-John back in the 70s. Each time he came back to Australia, he came to see me, and I did a lot of arrangements and orchestrations for him. He was also an amazing performer on stage. He had an enormous amount of energy and would sweat buckets to give the best in his shows.

The last time we appeared together was in the concert for the opening of the Entertainment Centre. We were quite good friends; I remember he came to visit me in hospital after my heart surgery and I can recall him saying, 'Now don't you go and die on me; I've got lots more arrangements I need you to do.' He was a very talented man and he was generous and fun loving – a nice person. I was very sorry to see him go.

In the 70s, I was fortunate to do a tour with Perry Como and he was one of the most delightful people I have worked with. He was a real professional and one of the calmest, least flappable people I have ever met. He was so laid-back and so relaxed: nothing ever bothered him.

The tour was a huge one. We started in Sydney, then went to Melbourne, Perth and finally back to Melbourne. The first concert was at the Sydney Opera House. On the day of the first concert we had rehearsed with the orchestra and the back up singers, and Perry wanted to hear what it sounded like. And so he said, 'Tommy, come with me,' and we went into the auditorium and sat down about twenty rows back to listen. He was toying with this huge flashy diamond ring he was wearing, and in the process, he slipped it off his finger and accidentally dropped it. He didn't panic: he just mildly said, 'Oh, I've just dropped my diamond ring'. 'That's okay,' I said, thinking it couldn't have rolled far. 'We'll look for it.'

Well, it took us five hours and an army of people. Everyone else was panicking – it was getting late and the audience was about to come in. There were ushers everywhere, scouring the floor. He was totally unfazed. He just shrugged and said, 'Don't worry, they'll find it,' and they did, about ten minutes before the doors were due to open for that evening's performance.

By the time we got to Adelaide, there was great camaraderie among the whole group. Musicians, singers, technicians – Perry knew most of them by name. There were four boys and four girls in the backing group, and they were kicking their heels up. We were back stage at the Festival Theatre in Adelaide, preparing for the opening night show; the girls were in one dressing room, the boys were across the hall and Perry's dressing room was at the end of the corridor. There was a lot of hilarity going on: the boys knocking on the girls' dressing room while they were dressing, the girls squealing. There was a lot of giggling and running in and out of each other's dressing rooms in various stages of undress. The door at the end of the corridor opened and Perry put his head out and said, 'What's all the noise about?' My dressing room was next door and so hearing all this, I went out to quieten things down a bit. I told them to keep it down and not annoy Perry. It worked for a minute, then it was on again, lots of laughing and running about. And next thing, Perry's door opened again, and instead of the blast they were all expecting, Perry strolled out, totally naked! It was the young ones who were fazed that time.

We finished this tour in Perth, but it had been so popular that the organisers wanted to schedule another concert in Melbourne. Perry had the time and the orchestra was available and so straight after our final concert in Perth, the whole cast caught 'the red-eye special' back to Melbourne for another concert the following night. The plane left Perth about midnight and got into Melbourne about 5.00 or 6.00 a.m.

We were all ferried off to our hotel to catch up on some sleep, while the equipment was loaded into a semi-trailer to the Festival Hall. However, once he got there the driver left his truck for a moment while he found someone to open a loading bay, and his truck was stolen.

In typical fashion, Perry wasn't fazed by this at all. I was just getting ready to go to sleep and the phone rang. It was Perry who told me what had happened to our equipment. 'Don't worry,' he said, 'They'll probably find it before tonight. But if not, my son, I think you and I will do the concert. Just the two of us: I'll sing and you'll play the piano.' I was okay with that; I knew the performance back to front by then, but it still impressed me that he was so cool. He actually roared with laughter about the whole thing.

Chapter 11
Highlights

The MBE, Order of Australia, "This Is Your Life", Entertainment Centre Grand Opening, Vicky.

One of the proudest moments in my life was receiving the MBE – because, although it was presented by the Queen, it came from the Australian community. The great thing about it for me, was being accepted into a country that was not mine by birth and the feeling of having contributed something. I would have felt proud anyway, but being an adopted Australian, it made me feel even prouder. Not that I feel I'm adopted. I feel like I belong. In fact, I know I do, because I even enjoy cricket. I think it's marvellous. I love rugby and aussie rules but Eve still does not appreciate these sports.

We were living in Seaforth at the time and one day the phone rang as Eve came into my study. A voice on the end of the line said, 'This is Canberra calling,' and after a preliminary introduction the voice said, 'I would like to ask you if you would accept an honour?' I, of course, thought, 'I am going to be very careful here, in case this someone pulling my leg.'

I asked for the gentleman's name again: he was the secretary to the governor general. He realised that I was sceptical and so he assured me that I could check on his authenticity. Having sorted that out, he told me that my name was being nominated for an MBE and the reason that they were first checking with me was simply to avoid the embarrassing situation of having people refuse to accept it. I assured him that that would not be the case, and he rang off saying it would be followed up with a letter.

When I got off the phone, Eve was nodding, 'I thought so,' she said. She was pleased, but as for me, within minutes I had a migraine as big as a house. I was totally amazed, I couldn't believe that I would be given such an honour. I no longer thought of myself as a foreigner – I had been an Australian citizen for many years, but still, I was amazed that someone who was not born here, would be so totally accepted by this country.

That's what was so important: that it was an honour not just from the Queen and the Government, nor from the people who nominated me, but from the community which I had adopted and who had adopted me. For service to the performing arts. The process, I discovered later, was started by Mel, my manager. He had to have six people who would nominate me and so he approached a number of people including, the General Manager of 2CH, the General Manager of the Opera House and the Premier, Neville Wran.

I was so stunned: it was really only at the ceremony, when the award was handed to me, that it sunk in that it was a great occasion, one of my proudest moments. Eve and my young daughter Vicky were there and they were so proud. It was tremendous.

Ten years later I was awarded the Order of Australia. Again, it came out of nowhere, totally unexpected. And so they were proud moments for me but there were proud moments also in achieving things in the entertainment industry. For instance, in 1975, there was a program called, 'This Is Your Life'. That was wonderful too. It was a thrill and a real honour because this was only done for people who were very well known and would be instantly recognisable to the audience watching at home. Until then, I had no real sense of myself as a public identity. It showed me that I was better known then I thought.

Mel's partner, Bob Gun, rang me and said he had made an appointment for us to see the manager of the Opera House late on the following Friday and that he would pick me up. That was fine by me, and when the time came, he arrived and I was dressed very casually. He looked at me and said, 'Oh, Tommy, you can't go like that!' and ordered me off to get changed. I grumbled a lot, thinking it was a bit much to have to dress up for a simple meeting, but eventually I gave in and went and put on a shirt and tie and a jacket. He drove me backstage and said, 'You go on up to the green room and wait for me while I park the car.' Which I dutifully did, not suspecting anything was out of the ordinary.

I still didn't suspect not even when June Bronhill came in and greeted me. It was not entirely out of the ordinary for her to be there, and as she said while we were chatting, she had just finished a performance. There were people coming and going and I could see some commotion happening behind me but I paid it no attention: after all, in the Opera House green room it's all showbiz, there are always things happening. The next thing I knew, there were lights, and Digby Wolfe leaned over from behind with cameras around him and said, 'Tommy, this is your life.'

I was absolutely non-plussed for a moment. But, this is where the experience of thinking on your feet comes in to play, because I realised this was being recorded, and so, without even thinking of it, the other Tommy Tycho, the showbiz Tommy, automatically took over and I behaved as expected. I enjoyed it immensely. A car was waiting to take me to Channel Seven where everyone else was waiting to do the rest of the show.

One of the highlights was that they had flown my elder daughter and my granddaughter in from Iran. I had no idea they were coming. Eve and Vicky were in on it and I realised this at once. It also explained a frantic phone call I had from Vicky earlier in the day. 'Where's mum?' she had asked and when I said she was in town shopping, Vicky had said, 'Oh, never mind,' and hung up. 'Teenagers!' I thought at the time, with a shrug. But what had happened was that Dory had missed a connection and had not been on the plane when they had gone to pick her up, and Vicky was frantically trying to find out what had happened. As it turned out, Dory arrived on the next flight, but without her luggage. Eve rang and said she was still stuck in town when, in fact, they were all off buying Dory something to wear. And so all this flurry of activity was happening around me, and I was totally unaware of it. I was working on an orchestration that day, and, if anything, I was a little annoyed at all the interruptions. It was lovely that so many people took so much time to make that show.

The opening of the Entertainment Centre was another highlight in my career. It was an enormous show and I still regard it as a major achievement: a three and a half hour performance, with a big orchestra and almost 2,000 people on stage at the finale. It was simply enormous. The producer was Peter Faiman, who directed the first Crocodile Dundee film for Paul Hogan.

One of the best times of my life was when I was working with my daughter Vicky. This was in the 70s. Vicky has even more of a sense of entertainment than I have. I called her 'The Female Liberace' – that is the kind of flair she has. She was a very competent musician. When she was about six, she was pounding away on the piano one day and I asked her if she would like to learn the piano. She was adamant. 'Noooooooo!' she said, and that was okay with me. There was no sorrow in my heart that she had refused.

At around about eight years of age, having forgotten that incident completely, she came to me and asked me if she could learn and so I found her a teacher. I never for a moment considered teaching her myself – it was not so much a matter of not having the time but the belief that there a few things a man should never do. One is to teach piano to his children; the other is to teach his wife to drive a car: both are just asking for trouble. I was always there to observe her progress, to advise and guide her when she came asking questions, but the truth is, I am not a very good teacher. I cannot teach; I have no curriculum in my head.

And so Vicky started learning from the 'lady around the corner'. She went there for a couple of years, and one day this lady rang and asked me if I would come and see her. I thought, 'Oh dear, does this mean Vicky has been misbehaving?' But what she said was that Vicky was so good, she really needed special teaching. And so then I went to the conservatorium; Vicky was barely ten, and she was invited to apply to the high school attached to the conservatorium. They had an enormously high standard of entry and very few were accepted and, of course, those that were were the very best. They had 800-1,000 applications every year – and she made it. We were very proud.

As a student there, she was required to have a piano teacher. The celebrated pianist Isidor Goodman, one of the best ever in this country and a man of huge international standing, was a friend of mine and so I rang him and asked if he would teach her. When I told him her age, he paused and said, 'I'm sorry Tommy, but, even as a friend, I have to tell you, I don't teach beginners.' And so I asked him if he would just listen to her. He readily agreed, and so I took Vicky to him. I was waiting outside for ten minutes, then twenty minutes – after an hour they came out, and he simply said, 'I'll teach her.'

Many years later, she told me how difficult it had been, being my daughter and doing music. It meant living in my shadow to some extent; there was always something to measure up to. As a teenager it must have been very hard for her, although she never complained of it at the time. Eventually, she finished her studies with Isidor, and completed her time at the conservatorium, and she didn't want to see the piano ever again.

Having seen the promise in her ability, I was disappointed; not overwhelmingly so, however, and I thought I hid it very well. After all, her happiness was paramount. Then one day, at one of the annual Mo award presentation concerts, I did something unusual. This was in the early years of the Mo awards, but even then they were excellent, quite amazing productions. They are the major performing arts awards in Australia, and even now, the television channels are still not interested in televising them. It's a huge pity, because the performances are really quite spectacular. This one, seventeen years ago, was no exception.

We had ten pianos on stage playing a big roaring piece, a whole lot of songs in a medley. At first there were just two pianos at the front of the stage in front of the curtain – Geoff Harvey and me, in a musical battle. Then the curtain went up revealing the other eight pianos – four on my side, four on Geoff's side. It was a huge success, very theatrical. Vicky and Eve were in the audience and when we were driving home that night Vicky said to me, 'The next time you do that piece, I would like to play one of the pianos.' I nearly drove off the road. 'Sure,' I said.

As an aside, I should point out that Geoff Harvey and I are friends. There is a manufactured friendly rivalry between us which is concocted. When I was at Channel Seven as conductor, in the early years before I was musical director, I worked with Paul Hogan on his Specials. They proved so popular that he was offered a lucrative deal with Channel Nine and he moved across to that station. He asked me to continue to do his show, and I warned him it would not go down too well at Channel Nine. 'Never mind,' he said, and so I did the first show with them in Melbourne. That was the only one I did. I got a phone call soon after and he said, 'You were right, that didn't go down well at all.' And so we parted company, and Geoff Harvey took over the shows. We are virtually contemporaries. He started a bit later than I did, in the mid-sixties, and so I have ten years on him. But because we were both musical directors of rival stations there was always going to be that kind of rivalry. I have a lot of respect for him: he is a very competent musician and a good composer. He has written a lot of things that people are familiar with: Channel Nine logos and the music for 'The Sullivans,' the type of thing that everyone knows but would rarely attribute to Geoff.

Anyway, a few weeks later, I got a phone call from Hugh Cornish, who was then General Manager of Channel Nine asking me to produce and conduct a Royal Command Variety Performance in the following year. It was suggested that we repeat the ten pianos thing, with myself and Hugh, who was also an accomplished pianist, in the feature roles. 'On one condition,' I said. 'My daughter Vicky must be one of the pianists.' I came back and said to Vicky, 'You're on.' She said, 'Shit dad, I guess I better start practicing.' And so Vicky's first public performance was for the Queen.

The concert and the duelling pianos performance were a roaring success. That's what started the idea of the two of us performing together. Some time later we did a record for K-tel, and it was great – we enjoyed making it. Vicky and I appeared on every form of media, in most capital cities, at one time or another – television, radio, you name it: we talked up a storm of interest in that record.

On one occasion we were on a Sydney radio station, 2GB, at midnight. The DJ was a wonderful man called Owen Delaney. We were there for an hour and when we finished we came down stairs to find my car had been stolen. It was an absolutely dreadful night, pouring with rain, and there we were – stuck. I was with Eve and Vicky and her husband, and they said to me, 'Perhaps you parked it around the corner,' but I knew I hadn't. I pressed the intercom buzzer for 2GB, and Owen answered it. 'Owen,' I said, 'My car's been stolen.' 'Oh, my God,' he said. He put a record on and came down to let us in.

As we were talking about calling the police, he said, 'Hang on,' and raced back up to the studio, where he interrupted the record and announced over the air, saying that while we had been doing the interview that had just gone to air some bloody mongrel had stolen our car. He gave a description of it and he called on all the police, the taxi drivers, the truck drivers, everyone who was out, to look out for it and to ring us at 2GB if anyone saw it.

In the meantime, Vicky's husband said he was going to look around for it. I said, 'Glen, don't be stupid, it's still pouring with rain,' but he wandered off anyway, only to come belting back a few minutes later, saying, 'I've found it!' It was several blocks away with two guys in it trying to start it. Owen told us to stay where we were and he took off like a rocket, but the rest of us followed anyway as the rain was beginning to ease. When we arrived there was Owen, dragging these two guys out of the car and bashing them furiously. Finally the cops arrived, and I think it was actually a relief to these two guys. It appeared they had put a brick through the window, taken the handbrake off, and rolled it down the street where they were having trouble starting it because they were out to it with drugs. They hadn't reckoned with Owen, however, he had taken it personally. It was as if he felt we were his guests and he was incensed that our car had been stolen. And so there he was, a big athletic man, bashing them to billy-oh!

I believe the record we made had great potential to sell, but unfortunately, K-tel's marketing let us down. At the time, they were on the verge of bankruptcy and so the initial pressing of 10,000 or so was all they did. It was enormously disappointing because we could have sold many many more. It was so frustrating – we had people going into shops and saying 'Where can I get this?' and it simply wasn't available. On a positive note: from the strong media interest, we started to do concerts with the symphony orchestras around the country – Perth, Adelaide, Sydney, Tasmania, Melbourne, Brisbane, you name it – and they were hugely successful because Vicky was such a bright button. She had her confidence by then and she was a damn good pianist. She was a real entertainer and eventually, after the first half a year or so, she said, 'Dad I feel trapped behind the piano,' I asked what she wanted to do and she said, 'I want to sing.' We set up a couple of numbers that she could do in her own style, and she killed them with it, to use an old show business expression.

Then we did a concert tour in South Australia with a singer called Neil Williams; we were driving through all those beautiful country towns. A year earlier we had done a similar tour through northern Queensland from Townsville to Cairns. Eve was the roadie, and we had such a lot of fun. We saw places and met people we would never have had the opportunity to see or meet in any other way. And we brought a quality of entertainment to those towns that they were not used to, and they were so appreciative. It was wonderful but it was hard yakka. We did concerts in the morning for the senior citizens and then drove on in the afternoon. It wasn't a restful holiday, but it was a great experience. It was extremely well planned and my only requirement that at every venue we should have two perfectly tuned, good quality pianos. Which we did. Country people were far more hospitable and far more enthusiastic than any city audiences I ever met.

Vicky and I played together for many years. During that time her marriage had ended in divorce, it was one of those things that happen. She met David and fell head over heels in love with him. At that point she made a decision that the demands of the travel and the commitments were no longer suitable for her. I understand that and I fully accept and respect that decision. I am not disappointed because I believe she is doing what she wants to do now, which is being with her beloved husband David and planning a family. She remains a most professional musician. She has an incredibly keen ear and a strong connection with the show business tradition. As a youngster, she was always backstage doing things, helping Julie Anthony dress. Having gone from the back room to the front of stage she knows, from her own experience, how a performer ought to act on stage. She is an enormously constructive critic: it's a joy to discuss things with her. Like her mother and myself, she is an absolute film buff – there is nothing she doesn't know about films.

It is still, the greatest pleasure and joy to see one's own flesh and blood out there on the stage, absolutely "killing" the audience. I took a back seat when we performed together; my style was always more low-key than hers while she was nearly over-the-top, which an audience loves anyway. She was a dynamic performer, and for me to be there and conduct the orchestra, or to play piano with her was wonderful. I don't think there is a greater satisfaction in a person's life than to see one's offspring succeed, and so I have great and momentous memories of that association. Eve often says that Vicky, with her talent, should be a world star. But I say that she chose not to be. We are both happy. But it was a beautiful, marvellous period of time, because there was an inexplicable aura of charisma and incredible vibrations between two people. Now, that would have been there whether she was my daughter or not, but because she was my daughter, it was even better.

I have had this experience with just a few artists – Barry Crocker, Julie Anthony, Jackie Love, Don Cant and my new protege, Penny Hay. Simon Gallagher is another one. It doesn't happen often because you have to be on the same wavelength, you have to be soulmates in musical terms. With people like these, even though we don't see each other for ages, we can get together for a performance and it works like clock-work. It's great, and it has something to do with relaxing, they know I am 200 per cent behind them and so they relax and get on with it.

Live concerts, especially with artists like these with

whom I have such a rapport, are a real joy to me. Particularly lately, it is the area of my work that seems to have blossomed. The joy I get from it is, in fact, only surpassed by writing orchestrations. And that's because, I don't just "write orchestrations", I create a new song out of an existing one. I take a thirty-two bar pop song and recompose it. I add spice and drama and surprises so that it is made for the artist who will perform it. Before I orchestrate it, I rehearse it with the artist, and I tailor it so that it is a specially written song that becomes a party piece for them, and eventually they build up a repertoire of songs made just for them: no-one else sings them like that, or performs them like that. That is the best part, the creativity: to take an ordinary piece of sheet music, thirty-two bars with a melody and lyrics, and create a completely new thing out of it.

Chapter 12
Open Heart Surgery

I had a quadruple heart bypass operation in 1980 because of chronic angina. The angina attack is a debilitating thing: you are suddenly enervated, and you become so listless that you can hardly lift your arms. You're not unconscious although it's a bit like fainting, not like a heart attack and not as painful, but nearly as bad in terms of your health. It occurs because the arteries are blocked and, because they are choked, blood and oxygen are prevented from getting around the heart.

I suppose I should have been aware of what was going on, and now I am conscious of my health, but at the time, I was not prepared for it. Because I smoked around eighty cigarettes a day – a four-pack habit I had – I thought it was just the cigarettes playing havoc with my system. (I started smoking about thirty or fourty years ago: one, then two, then ten, then twenty, and so it just built up. The profession I'm in creates a certain amount of tension and in those days, when all my colleagues and everyone around me lit up and I just did too.) It was just a silly habit, which now, as a reformed smoker, I find more ridiculous than ever.

Strangely though, I never did smoke much at home, but whenever I was working, in a studio, between rehearsals, it was just something everyone did. You could, of course, smoke everywhere in those days, and so while I was rehearsing, I kept the packet beside me and just lit one after the other. I did switch to a pipe at one point, but it was too much trouble, and that didn't last long. I first realised how evil the habit was when I got nicotine poisoning. It wasn't pleasant. I was driving home late one night, well past midnight. I had been working long hours and smoking a lot and, obviously, I had just overloaded my body. I felt bile rise in my throat and pulled over just in time to avoid spoiling my brand new Mercedes. I sat in the car and for the next twenty minutes or so I couldn't move; waves of nausea washed over me. I was very ill. Finally it subsided and I was able to get home, and in the morning the doctor called. He took one sniff of me and said that I had poisoned myself with nicotine. I felt absolutely vile and I didn't touch a cigarette for over a year and a half: until a family crisis arose.

Eve's first daughter Dory lived in Teheran and Dory's second child was an absolutely beautiful girl called Pardis, which means Paradise. She was taken ill suddenly with a mystery illness and within twenty-four hours she had died. She was about four years of age. Eve was distraught. I booked Eve, Vicky and myself on the plane that afternoon and we arrived after forty-eight hours of travelling. While we where there, in those bleak days of mourning, someone offered me a cigarette and, not thinking, I lit up.

Having had one cigarette, I was fully addicted again, and from one, I quickly went back to my old habit -- and even worse. If I worked in a studio all day from nine o'clock in the morning to eleven o'clock at night, I chain-smoked that whole time. To make matters worse, I also lived on strong black European coffee – not a good combination. And when I felt these symptoms of being listless and enervated I thought, 'Oh I must stop smoking and drinking so much coffee.'

Then came the great honour, in 1980, of being chosen

to conduct the Royal Command Performance at the Sydney Opera House. This was the most amazing thing that I had done in my career. It was huge. Being on Channel Nine, it would have been logical for Geoff Harvey to be asked to be the musical director. But Peter Faiman, who was the director, rang and invited me to do it because of my previous experience and because of the enormous size of the task. It was the most exciting project I had ever been involved with.

I immediately took two week's holiday. Eve and I went to Honolulu and lay in the sun. I relaxed because I knew that would be my last chance for a long time. And on our return, it happened exactly as I thought; it was full on. I worked a staggering number of hours every day, orchestrating, arranging, and planning. It was the first Royal Command Performance ever held in Australia, and it was to be televised live on Channel Nine, across Australia.

It was a full two hour concert, and the challenge was to present it as a top class show to 2000 or more people in the Concert Hall, including the Royal Couple, and at the same time, televise it successfully so that the people at home would enjoy it too. A show like that is usually either a television show or it's a theatrical show: the two do not combine readily because the cameras get in the way and lights are far more strident in a television format than in a theatrical format. And so these difficulties had to be overcome.

We had a huge eighty piece orchestra, and on the night, when the Royal Couple arrived, the orchestra was to play God Save The Queen. Because this was a preliminary opening, it could be conducted by my assistant conductor and I was to come on stage after it to begin the show. While this was happening, I was waiting in the wings and felt this searing pain in my heart, and I thought, 'Oh no, not now please!' After a while it went away and because of the elation I was feeling and the anticipation of what I was about to do, I soon forgot about it but at the time it was as if a sword had been driven through my heart.

A few weeks later, Don Lane rang me in a panic: his musical director had been taken ill and he wanted me to help out. Don and I go back a long way, and so I went to Melbourne to do his show that night. What was originally a one-off, just helping out, became a regular stint. And so for about two and a half months, I flew to Melbourne to do the Don Lane show from Monday to Friday and then I flew back to Sydney where I had other commitments on the weekends. I was working at a frantic pace and on top of it all, Don said, 'While I've got you here I want to do a record,' and so, sandwiched in between all the other things, we started to put together an album of about fourteen songs with orchestration.

After about two and a half months, I was relieved of my temporary post as musical director on the show, but continued to work on the album which was still planned to be recorded in Melbourne. I wrote the last arrangement at my desk one morning; I wrote the last note of the last arrangement and then I fainted. Eve came in and found me and called the doctor who called the ambulance and I was rushed straight to hospital. I was given the whole run of tests but they couldn't find anything and so I was moved to the ward and told I could go home the next morning.

I recall, the next morning my doctor telling me that I'd given them a scare but that I was okay. Then I fainted again. That's all I recall, but I know that they whisked me back into intensive care, gave me an angiogram and discovered that I had four major blockages in the arteries leading to my heart, two of them completely blocked. Over the next few days my condition got worse and my scheduled surgery was brought forward. In those days the operation took about six hours. It was done by a team of doctors led by the very famous surgeon, and friend of mine, Victor Chang.

Fifteen years ago, this was a major operation, and the recuperation period was a lot longer. Both physically and mentally, it was the greatest shock to my system that I have ever experienced. I was kept in hospital for about two weeks afterwards, and once I was allowed home, it took six weeks for me to recuperate to the point where I could walk around. It took me a lot longer to get completely back to normal. For four years after that I was mentally a bit shaky. Every time I had the slightest pang of pain in my body, I panicked. If I had wind, I panicked. It took me four years to get over the shock of having such a narrow escape from death; it was like being shown how mortal I was. There were times, travelling to Melbourne, for instance, when everything was fine until the door closed in the hotel room and I was on my own. Then I couldn't sleep. I would panic. It was a helpless feeling – what if something happened when I was here alone?

One day, I was to do a concert with Vicky in Newcastle and we were to fly there. As the plane took off, I paled – not because of the flight but because I felt a pain in my chest. I coughed and I felt it again. All during the flight I sweated. Vicky, sitting next to me, held my hand and said, 'Its okay. You'll be okay,' but I was so scared. I felt dreadful. When we finally got off the plane I was pale and shaken. We went straight to the hotel and I rested, and when I woke, I was fine. I was as good as gold.

That made me realise something: soon after that it happened again, in the middle of the night, and I woke feeling a pain, and thought instantly 'Oh no, not now, not again!' but then I started thinking, 'What the hell; it's four years down the road and nothing has happened I'm okay. I will be okay'. And from then on I was. Looking back now, I can see that it was simply a process of adjusting, and that my fear had played havoc with me. I had never been afraid of anything in my life and then suddenly I was. I was working all through this time, and when I was working I was fine, but the moment I was left alone, in the car driving or at night when everything was quiet – night has got this awful habit of magnifying all the problems of the world – then I got scared and panicky.

It is interesting to compare this experience with the operation I had two years ago, which only took about two and a half hours as opposed to six. I was walking three days after I was operated on. I also knew what to expect and so I was better prepared to handle it. When I'd had the first operation which included four bypasses, Victor Chang warned me that these would not last forever. 'If you are very unlucky,' he said 'they may need replacing in about eight years. If you are very lucky, it may be as long as sixteen or seventeen years.'

And so, after ten years had passed, I was aware that the problem could arise: but no symptoms appeared and so I kept on as normal. I didn't have any symptoms right up until the time that we finished the Anthony Warlow concert. It was a killer of a tour -- we had two concerts in Brisbane, five in Melbourne, six in Sydney, three in Adelaide and two in Perth, all within twenty-one days. In every new city I had to rehearse with a new orchestra as well, and so it was a gruelling schedule. I don't suggest for a second that that was the reason for my heart attack, but it certainly helped speed it up. I finished the tour on the Sunday, flew home, and on Thursday I had the heart attack. Fortunately, it was a minor heart attack, but I do recall that the pain was unbearable. I kept lapsing into unconsciousness. An angiogram revealed that this time there were two arteries blocked and a third one partially blocked, and so I was operated on again, to replace the original grafts. This time, I asked the doctors how long the bypasses would last, 'Twenty years,' they said, and I replied that that would do me.

I was due to go to surgery first thing in the morning. The nurse offered me a sleeping pill the night before, but I refused it. I slept fine without it. And so, both physically and mentally, I coped much better the second time.

My recovery was not as smooth as I had hoped however; within weeks of coming home from hospital I began to have trouble with my prostate gland. It was a condition not uncommon with men in my age group, but it quickly became so serious that I found myself back in hospital for another operation, barely three weeks after the bypass.

In the meantime, I had a concert planned with Julie Anthony and Anthony Warlow, at the Opera House. It began to look as if I wouldn't make it, but I did. – to a standing ovation from the audience. It also made the national news, and for the first time it truly sunk in for me that I was known and liked throughout the country. It was a good feeling, knowing that so many people genuinely cared for my wellbeing. All my life, my focus had been within my home, my family and my work, and I had never really thought of myself as exceptional or even as a public identity.

I had a similar feeling while doing the concert tour with Anthony Warlow. My name wasn't mentioned in the promotions and advertisements for the concerts. It just said, 'Anthony Warlow in Concert.' I was disappointed; I felt I had a big enough name to rate a mention. But it was already done, and there was nothing I could do about it.

I discussed it with my manager Ken Laing, and he said, 'Look I can understand your disappointment, but you have always been a professional and you have committed yourself to this and I think your integrity won't allow you not to do it'. He was right, and so although I wasn't pleased about it, I got on with it.

As it turned out, there was a full house everywhere we went. The tour was a total sell-out, and each time, when the orchestra came on stage and I walked up to the podium, I received huge applause because the audience didn't realise I was going to conduct. It was very gratifying. I must also say that Anthony also gave me all the accolades he could during and at the end of each concert.

After a bypass operation, if you follow a healthy diet and lifestyle, you have a good future ahead, there are no real restrictions on your life. I try to follow a fairly regulated life: I have breakfast in the mornings – very Spartan, something like a cup of tea and some toast; we have a light lunch – salad or sandwiches; and a main meal in the evening. I avoid fat, I don't eat eggs and I eat red meat only rarely. And so my diet is now largely fruit and vegetables, fish and chicken and occasionally a sweet. Victor Chang gave me this advice. I told him I had a sweet tooth and he said, 'Well, it's okay to have sweets, just don't make a habit of it.' I have a relatively healthy lifestyle now too. I walk everyday for at least an hour and in the summer I like to swim daily too. It's a lifestyle that I should have adopted when I was much younger! I feel more energetic and there is more virility in my work than ever in my life – that only happens when you feel really good about yourself.

In recent years, perhaps as a substitute for the excesses of my youth, I've discovered another vice – although, I don't think it is a vice but more of a diversion – and that is a love of card playing. My wife, and my entire family – every part of it, including my mum – were absolutely mad keen card players. I had always pulled out of playing cards: it didn't interest me and I thought it was a waste of time. And so usually I was doing other things while they were playing. I would quite happily drive Eve to our friends' places for card games and I would return at midnight or later to pick her up, or stay there and watch television. Until the first bypasses, when according to Eve, Victor Chang not only operated on my heart, but also my brain, because from that moment onwards, I became an inveterate card player.

I love it. I realised that I couldn't be locked into music every moment of every day and that I had to somehow divorce myself from it for small stretches of time. Playing cards, I found, was very good for this because it made me concentrate on something else. We now have a lot of friends who live near us, and we visit each other's places for cards. I never realised how much fun it was.

I also admit to having a 'square eye'. I watch television avidly – to the chagrin of my wife. According to her, whenever we come home, whether it's day or night, the first thing I do, even before I turn the light switch on, is turn on the television . Eve is a movie buff, but she is not the television addict that I am. And when I don't want to do anything I just plonk myself down in front of it, any time in the afternoon or evening. In the mornings, I always have a million things to do, and so I don't watch television then, but sometimes, in my study, I will turn it on anyway with the volume down low and have it on for company. If something really interesting takes my eye, I will stop to watch for a while.

I like to know what's happening in the industry, but more than that, for me it's purely entertainment. It relaxes me, it takes me out of myself and lets me turn off from any high pressure job I may be working on. I'll watch anything – football, movies, even one that's half way through. Eve will come in and say, 'What is happening?' and I will say, 'I have no idea,' but I'll watch it through to the end anyway.

Unlike the cards, this is not a recent thing. I think I became addicted to television from the moment it began, in the 50s. When I travel, wherever I am, whether Perth or Auckland, if I wake up early the first thing I do is turn on the television and watch whatever is on. If it's interesting I watch it right through; if it's boring it sends me back to sleep and so it's a bit of double benefit. I really can't live without a television set.

The first bypass operation was a significant catalyst for change in my life. I think that when one goes through a kind of trauma like that, it is life-changing. For the first time I had a lot of time to myself, to think, which I never had time for before. I was forced to lie in bed recuperating, doing very little, and doing absolutely nothing connected with working. I had the chance to think and to rationalise things and all of a sudden I thought, 'What the hell am I chasing? Why am I running wildly, working high-pressure, long-hour weeks?' It was certainly no longer necessary for financial security because by then we were secure. I suddenly realised I was killing myself. And for what? That realisation made me slow down a bit.

I still have times when projects overlap – one is late, the other has taken longer to complete than I hoped – and the deadlines force me to burn the candle at both ends again. My integrity requires me to deliver the best results

I can, and so I think this is sometimes unavoidable. But it's not as often as it used to be – despite the fact that Eve says I'm working as hard as I used to. I do work – I cannot go one day in my life without doing something constructive, even if it is only ten minutes' work – but I also have time to play cards, to visit friends and to go to the movies. It's time I didn't have before.

Eve still thinks I am working too hard. In the past, I didn't have a private life: I worked, I fell into bed, I got up and worked. I don't really know, even now, what was driving me all those years. I know there was a motor running and I had to keep up. I suppose subconsciously I needed to build a security into my life. Because I came here with virtually nothing and had to establish an existence, and then I had the responsibility of a family, it kept on going, until I found myself on a treadmill that took over, and the pace just accelerated.

It got so that I was hardly even aware of the financial gain. It was simply the fact that I felt I had to achieve one thing, and then another, to take another step forward. I think the unconscious drive was a personal one: I felt that I had to establish myself. I suppose it's a natural human desire to better yourself, and so, from one performance to another, as success started to come, it just went on building.

If I try to analyse it, I'm sure that the experience of loosing the stability of my early life in Hungary is connected. It made me more conscious of wanting security. But perhaps I would have been the same, even without that experience. There is something in me that I am not aware of, or rather, I know what it is but can't describe it: it has to do with discipline, the self-discipline that has been built in to my life since I was a kid. If I don't do anything, I feel guilty. The only time I don't is when I'm on holidays, and then it depends on how tired I am. I can usually, rest for a week – maybe two if I'm very tired – but then I start to feel energetic again and I' become eager to get back to work. It's that self-discipline that drives me to work everyday because if I didn't work I'd feel useless. It's the thing that gives shape to my life.

I don't consciously think about the values I hold. I'm not a wowser. I have certain morals, because of my central European background and I'm fairly liberal in my thinking. I don't condemn much – except crime which I hate. But I do know that money is not important to me and it has never been a motivator for me. I have been fortunate in that, all my life, I have not needed to work for money to feed my family. As a child I had the security of my family, and later as an adult. I had this amazing earning capacity. And so I have always had enough money. On the other hand, I have not wanted to own a yacht or a plane. But I have a good life. I am useless with money – in our household, it is Eve who is the Minister of Finance and it has never been a motivator for me. I also think that the experience of the holocaust and the horror that I saw then, has affected my perspective. I know that, in the end, worldly goods don't mean anything. I don't penny-pinch; I don't have the time or the energy or the interest to shop around, to save a few dollars. I just know that, having achieved a certain plateau, I then had to do more, do better with my work, to achieve the next step.

Earlier in my life, I was jealous of other people's successes. It's a human trait, and one I am ashamed of; but I was envious. When I heard about a project that was given to someone else, it would gnaw at me and I would think 'Why? Why wasn't it offered to me?' I wanted to do it all. That is something that disappeared after the first bypass operation. It was as if, at that time, I rationalised what I had achieved in my life and I concluded that having achieved all these things there was no need for me to be jealous of other people's successes. I realised that I didn't have to be greedy wanting everything all the time, and that there were other people who were equally as talented, if not more so, and they also deserved opportunities. And so my jealousy disappeared. That three months of recuperation changed a lot of things for me.

One thing that has become very important to me in these later years is the sharing of my experience and knowledge with others.

About eight years ago, Ken Laing my manager came to me and said, 'Tommy, at this point in your life, it's time you started to put something back into the industry, to pass on the benefits of your experience.' And he was right. I was so locked into my daily routine of doing things all the time that I did not think to look at other opportunities. It was Ken who started me doing things like the patronages. I genuinely like to do things that will help others, even before I was involved in these official patronages, I would always do what I could to help people. Sometimes it meant I would go flat to the board, trying to get everything done, and Eve would say, 'Can't you learn the simple word "No"?' But if it was a colleague, or someone who needed my help, I couldn't refuse. She was always angry at me and said, 'You must sometimes stop and think of yourself!' This was long before I accepted any official positions, and now my time is regulated, but the patronages still keep me busy, because to me it's not just a matter of accepting an honour and having my name on the letterhead: it means a fair amount of work too.

The first appointment I had was as the patron of the

Pan Pacific Music Camp. Every year in January, kids from all over the Pacific area get together for ten or twelve days to learn and to play music. They have a great time. They make lots of friends and they learn a great deal. It's exciting, and eight years later I am still the patron. It's the most exciting thing to see those high school kids, who are all good musicians individually, come together and eat, drink and sleep music. They learn to work together in choirs and bands and orchestras and string quartets, and at the end of the camp they perform in a great concert. The first rehearsals are terrible but by the end, they are brilliant.

I am also patron of the Australian entertainment Mo awards – named after Mo, who, by legend, was the greatest Australian comic – which started as a little suburban award for artists and performers who appeared in clubs and the like. It was started by Don Lane and Johnny O'Keefe. It has now grown and has been extended to include everything – opera, theatres, circus, symphony orchestras, buskers, everything. Ken Laing is chairman, and I am patron. We are trying to take it beyond its Sydney base to become a truly national award that acknowledges and encourages excellence in all areas of the performing arts similar to the Oscars in Hollywood. I think it is important for this country to have such an award, and that's why I accepted this appointment. Again, I felt it was an enormous accolade, for me to be asked.

I have another appointment as artistic patron of the Sydney Cultural Council, which is the governing body of the Macdonalds Performing Arts Challenge. (It used to be called the City of Sydney Eisteddford. It has been around for about 60 years.) I was asked to be an artistic patron, after many years of being a judge. They were trying to lift the profile of the event by associating it with known names and personalities, and I accepted because I could see that here was a chance to do something with this stale old musty organisation and lift it into the Twentieth Century.

The Performing Arts Challenge is so important because these young people are the future. We are trying to encourage them to develop, and there is nothing healthier than competition, pitting yourself against someone else's talents. Even if you lose, the competition is what's important because it gives you an edge, an adrenalin buzz, and makes you set goals. Even the rock bands benefit. Rock is not normally disciplined and to succeed in these environments, you need discipline.

And so with Ken, who has such a brilliant, vital brain, we decided the event had to be renamed. Eisteddfod is from the Welsh and means excellence in performance, but we felt it was an old-fashioned idea. We struck a lot of opposition from the old-timers, but when a major sponsor pulled out they all shook their heads and said, 'What are we going to do' and that's when Ken and I said, 'Right, we are going to rename it so that it will be relevant for now and into the next century. And then we are going to go out and get new sponsors.' It's now called the Macdonald's Performing Arts Challenge and it is open to rock bands and all sorts of new people and types of music. The artistic patrons now also include Dame Joan Sutherland, Don Burrows, James Morrison and Maina Gielgud, and the credibility of the event has risen dramatically.

What the old guard couldn't understand was that we were not trying to abolish it, we were trying to update a grand and very eminent event. It had a spectacular history, and it was wonderful what it has achieved, but it needed to be suited to new era as well.

My impatience with the Sydney Eisteddfod people is

not a rebellion, it's different. I feel the same with the ABC; I find it bogged down in it's own importance. The people there have an attitude that says, 'Don't make waves. It's been good enough for sixty years or whatever, it's good enough for us for now.' But it's not. They're not developing, not growing, not rolling with it.

I find people like that are hamstrung by their own inability to see the world outside their little cocoon. They don't see the real world. It's an incestuous organisation. When I was younger, I would have liked to get in amongst them and change it, but at my age now I have very little idealism left. I don't mean to be defeatist but, at 67, you become aware that time is not unlimited and that changing an organisation like the ABC is a huge thing. It's just not what I would choose to put my time and energy into now.

When I look back on my life, there are times when I sincerely cannot believe the success I've had. It comes to me more and more in these, my older days – I am increasingly given awards and other acknowledgments and I simply cannot believe that a simple musician can achieve so much. Among my musical colleagues, okay, but to be recognised in the street, to be known by so many people outside of my profession, that amazes me because I think it's only something that happens to the front-of-stage performers -- singers and entertainers. Delightful as it is, it is a constant source of surprise to me.

I have a low self esteem but I am proud of what I have done. It is a matter of taking pride in my work and that makes me want to do better all the time. But it still surprises me that others are proud of my work too. I have never been able to accept the acknowledgments of others easily. I am often embarrassed by the awards I've been given. I am humbled when someone recognises me on the street and comments on my work. It is a compliment, but to get awards from my peers is, strangely, embarrassing. I battle with this situation all the time. I feel as if I do not deserve such recognition, and that there are far more people with more talent than I, who deserve it more. But at the same time I am thrilled to receive it and I accept it graciously.

That was a lesson I learned many years ago. In my early years, when I would do a performance or a concert, people would come up to me afterwards and say, 'That was terrific! You were great!' And I would say, 'No I wasn't, I was terrible. I made so many mistakes, I am ashamed of myself.' And then I would see disbelief on their faces and the look of admiration in their eyes would turn to anger. It was as if they were thinking, 'The stupid, ungrateful bastard, he doesn't deserve my compliment.' And so I learnt very early on that – even if I knew I had done poorly, it was churlish to not accept a genuine compliment graciously, because it was better to make people feel good than to tear them down.

I'm not one of those people who want to achieve things so that after they're dead people will remember them for this or that. I do not want to be remembered for doing anything extraordinary. I'm just doing a daily job I was obviously predestined to do, and I have enough pride in myself that I want to do the best I can on every occasion. I think that is probably the most satisfaction I can have out of life.

And so to the future. People often ask me what I still want to do in my life. All I can say is that I do not have a master plan, I'm rolling along with what happens. In recent years, I have been fortunate and indeed privileged to have conducted all the major orchestras in Australia, as a guest conductor, doing my own kind of program. That is, it's not classical music, it's music for millions. In the process, I have gained the friendship and respect and recognition of those musicians, and I would like to continue this association. It also gives me enormous joy to nurture and develop new young talent and help them to become recognised, and doing these kinds of concerts allows me to do that, by introducing new singers to the stage.

And so that is basically how I see my future at the moment. If I'm asked to do film scores or recordings I will find time for those as well. It's a lovely life at the age of 67, to be as active as I am, and I want to keep on being as active as I can for as long as I live.

Chapter 13
The Lives That Touch

I am very conscious that my achievements and my successes have been as the result of a lot of other people's help, hard work and good will. I have learned so much from so many people it would be an impossible task to begin to name them all. However, in some small way I would like to acknowledge the fact that so many people have been important to me.

I would like to give credit to those countless musicians I have had the privilege of working with over the years, the many individuals and many orchestras. There is one group in particular, which Ken Laing loosely calls the Sydney International Orchestra, which is a bunch of great people. They are not a regular orchestra but are usually available every time Ken calls them to do a recording or a concert.

There are all the symphony orchestra players whom I have grown to know and love over the many years in which we have worked together. These include musicians in New Zealand too – in Auckland, Christchurch and Dunedin.

Another group of people whom are seldom acknowledged are the sound engineers. In the past thirty-five or forty years I have worked with so many, that I couldn't name them all. They are the unsung heroes in this business. I would like them to know that I have valued their expertise, their input and their contribution.

There has also been an enormous number of radio and

TV personalities who have been very kind to me, and who have helped foster my career over the years. They have given me support, public recognition, and sympathetic publicity. And I would also include people like Mike Walsh and Ray Martin on this score, for all the times they mentioned me on The Midday Show, when they would jokingly remind Geoff Harvey that if he didn't keep in line, they could always get me to do his job. It all built a certain profile.

There are many special people in the industry who have been very good to me: Bert Newton, John Laws, Alan Jones, Brian Bury, Steve Raymond, John Pearce of Sydney's 2GB, and a lot of others. And people such as Don Lane and Graham Kennedy whom I worked with over many years.

There are many incredibly good friends and talented performers with whom I have had the pleasure of working from the very beginning. I have spoken about some of them at length. There are many others whom I have not talked about, but they are just as dear to me.

David Grey is one. He was a superb tenor, and over the years we made more than a dozen records together. Sadly, he died last year from a heart condition. He was diagnosed with it about the time I was recuperating from my first bypass operation. David rang me, and in the course of this conversation, he told me of his diagnosis. He also told me that it was inoperable. It was a very emotional conversation. He actually broke down and cried and because I was still so vulnerable, I found it hard to cope with.

Later, because it troubled me so much, I discussed it with Eve, and rang him back to convince him that he needed a second opinion. David was reluctant to question his doctor, but eventually I persuaded him to see Victor

Chang. Victor did operate, David had eight bypasses, which was amazing in those days, and he lived for another fourteen years. After that, when we worked together, David would joke that between us, we had twelve bypasses and that luckily, they all worked better than those connected to the freeways of whatever capital city we were in.

Peter Brandon and Mary Jane Boyd, were two singers whom I worked with on many occasions while doing the 2CH concert series. I would also like to mention Jackie Love, Kamahl, Rolf Harris, Diana Trask, Joan McInnes who has recently married Sir James Hardy, Barry Crocker, Don Cant and the many others with whom I was lucky enough to be involved with in their early careers. Two more are Penny Hay, with whom I am currently working, and Bernard Walz, a brilliant young pianist with whom I have recently made a record. At the record launch, I made a little speech and I called him 'my worthy successor'. I also pointed out that, like Prince Charles, however, he has to wait a little while!

Despite all these tremendous people in my life, the greatest tribute I could make would be to Eve. We have been married for forty-five years and our lives are intertwined. She has been very patient; to live with a person who is as committed as I am would not be an easy thing. I couldn't have married me! After all these years we have settled down into a pattern where she accepts that when I am working, I am working. Sometimes, if it gets late and I'm still working, she might come and remind me to eat, but she never has nagged me. Also, she herself has worked hard all her life, until about ten or twelve years ago when she decided she'd had enough. And so she understands the drive that gets you up in the morning, that sense of purpose that is found in work.

I don't know what else to say, it may come out wrongly if I say something about her. It is hard for me to put into words what I feel about her. She has been a great partner, she is part of my life. Eve is a very strong lady. She knows what she wants and she goes after it. She has a very determined mind. She has also supported me in so many ways in all the time I have known her.

My family is also very special to me. Both of my daughters and Dory's entire brood are very close to me. Since that first reunion, we have seen each other regularly, and we have also been to Iran several times. Dory's father ended up marrying again; he had several sons and he only passed away recently in Vancouver. He was intelligent and very handsome, but because he was so rich, he just had no sense of responsibility and was a playboy all his life. But when we were in Teheran, he received both Eve and myself with great civility.

Dory's youngest child, Cherie was born in Australia. Having lost a child, Dory was nervous during her pregnancy, and she wanted to be with us in Sydney. She stayed for six months. When Cherie was a teenager, Dory even sent her to high school here in Sydney, and then spent the next six years virtually commuting between Australia and Iran. Dory's husband is a cultured, intelligent man. He was educated in the USA and England, and is very open in his thinking. We have often tried to encourage him to settle here too, but he will not. He is a proud Iranian in spite of the flaws in the current regime. He believes his place is there with his people. But he travels, and has been to visit us several times.

Dory herself is fairly cosmopolitan. She comes here to Australia to go to theatres and restaurants and concerts and auctions – all of those things that the Ayatollah has banned. This is something of a haven to her, where she is free to enjoy these things.

I suppose my family is somewhat unusual. It really is a united nations and every religion is represented. Both Eve and I are Jewish. Our daughter Dory is Moslem, married to an Iranian. Vicky has married a real dinky-di Aussie who is Anglican. Our eldest granddaughter Bita married a German who is a Buddhist, and we have learned lately – and this is still unofficial – our youngest grandchild who is at university in Kent in England, is very interested in a young man who is Japanese and whom we assume would follow the Shinto religion.

There are also many many people who are dear to me because they helped to teach me my profession. I'd like to acknowledge the early influences of Leo Weiner and Egon Petri, and all the big name stars I was lucky enough to work with and learn from throughout my career.

In a professional sense, there are obviously many composers who influenced me. I went through the traditional classical training from Bach, Haydn, Mozart, and Beethoven, in my early days, in central Europe there was a dogmatic way of teaching. All these influences went through my brain virtually unbeknown to me. I always had a fascination with listening to orchestral music, and as a result I quickly got bored with the early classical musical styles because they didn't sufficiently give me the input I was craving for. And so early on in my career I developed a taste for studying, learning and enjoying the work of the more sophisticated composers from the post-classical period – Wagner, Chopin, Liszt, Schumann, Schubert and Mendelssohn. I also studied the early twentieth century composers like Debussy, Ravel, Stravinsky, Richard Strauss and so on, because they were so incredibly fascinating and sophisticated in their music and their style and orchestration, and this is what I have craved all my life. I have always devoured this kind of music, listening to the intricate orchestral colours, and I think my arrangements nowadays reflect all these influences.

In the end though, I find it hard to say who, other than my family members were really significant in my life, because I have always been a loner. I am able to talk to people and get along with just about everybody I've ever met, but I've never had a close friend – anyone that I would confide in. It's not something I miss; I've never felt the need for it and I've never felt that I've had anything to confide anyway. I have been a daydreamer all my life and sometimes life becomes a little unreal as a result of it.

But influences – well, that's different. A lot of people have touched my life. I have lots and lots of friends, acquaintances and colleagues. There are so many wonderful people around me, and I suppose that every one of them have influenced me in some way, perhaps even in ways unknown to me.

My musical education is still continuing. I listen to music in my spare time. Funny, I never have had much spare time but these days I make time If it's a sunny day, I sit out on the terrace for an hour and I listen to music. I don't listen to anything in particular. I can listen to anything, as long as it's well done. I can even listen to Hawaiian music. As long as it's in tune and well done, it gives me a lift.

Other titles available from Brolga Publishing:

By Hazel Hawke / A Little Bit Of Magic

By Denis Waitley
Psychology Of Winning / Hard cover edition
Seeds Of Greatness / Hard cover edition
The Treasure Within

By E. James Rohn
Five Major Pieces To The Life Puzzle
The Seasons Of Life
Treasury Of Quotes
Seven Strategies For Wealth And Happiness
Daily Reflections
Daily Reflections Journal

By Charles E. "T" Jones
The Books You Read / Business Edition
The Books You Read / Professional Edition

By W. Mitchell / The Man Who Would Not Be Defeated

By Peter McKeon / The Wish List

By Dr. Wayne Dyer / Gifts From Eykis

Nonna Morelli's Favourite Recipes
101 Benefits of Baldness
Money Saving Travel Tips
The Quadrant Solution
Motivation Magic
Reflections
A Light Heart Lives Long
Hooked On Golf
As A Cat Thinketh
Women On Men
Keep The Words Coming
A Bushie's Guide To Life
A Bushie's Guide To Christmas
Desperate, Dateless, Dangerous & Devious Diary 1996
Desperate, Dateless, Dangerous & Devious Address Book

Brolga Publishing titles are distributed in Australia by HarperCollins

Any enquiries or mail orders to:

Brolga Publishing Pty Ltd
c/o GPO Box 959, Ringwood, Victoria 3134, Australia.